The Curtiss-Bright Cities

Although, at first glance, the immediate thought of the viewer of this photo will likely be that it is simply a photograph of Miami taken in the early 1920s, looking south on Northeast Second Avenue at the point at which it crosses Thirty-sixth Street (and, indeed, that is what the scene appears to be), this image, in actuality, is a great deal more than that. If one looks just to the right of the "Miami Welcomes You" billboard, across Thirty-sixth Street one will see the "junior version" of the great thirty-something-foot-tall Indian icon, known variously as either Jack Tigertail or Chief Willy Willy (sometimes spelled with an "ie" at the end instead of a "y"), which graced Okeechobee Road and welcomed travelers to Hialeah for many years. Here, with his left arm extended to the west, pointing the way toward Hialeah, is Big Chief Potchentouchouss (Pot-chen-touchouss), the little brother of "the big guy" who was for so many years a Hialeah landmark. And with that our journey west and north of Miami begins.

The Curtiss-Bright Cities

Hialeah, Miami Springs & Opa Locka

Seth H. Bramson

Charleston   London

History
PRESS

Published by The History Press
Charleston, SC 29403
www.historypress.net

Cover image: The new and magnificent fountain and welcoming arch to the city of Hialeah, located at the city's southern entrance on Okeechobee Road.

Unless otherwise credited, all photographs are from the collection of the author.

First published 2008

Manufactured in the United Kingdom

ISBN 978.1.59629.386.1

Library of Congress Cataloging-in-Publication Data

Bramson, Seth, 1944-
The Curtiss-Bright cities: Hialeah, Miami Springs and Opa Locka / Seth
Bramson.
p. cm.
ISBN-13: 978-1-59629-386-1 (alk. paper)
1. Hialeah (Fla.)--History. 2. Hialeah (Fla.)--History--Pictorial works.
3. Miami Springs (Fla.)--History. 4. Miami Springs
(Fla.)--History--Pictorial works. 5. Opa Locka (Fla.)--History. 6. Opa
Locka (Fla.)--History--Pictorial works. 7. Curtiss, Glenn Hammond,
1878-1930. 8. Bright, James H., 1866-1959. 9. Florida--Biography. I.
Title.
F319.H49B73 2008
975.9'381--dc22
                              2007046015

Notice: The information in this book is true and complete to the best of our knowledge. It is offered without guarantee on the part of the author or The History Press. The author and The History Press disclaim all liability in connection with the use of this book.

The Curtiss-Bright cities have been blessed for a good few years with an equally good few people interested in preserving the history of the three communities. To their great credit, the folks in Miami Springs have gone so far as to establish a museum of the Curtiss-Bright cities' history, centering on Glenn Curtiss and Miami Springs but including all three municipalities. For many years, prior to the move to its own facility on Westward Drive, the museum was on the second floor of the Stadnik Drug Store "on the circle."

Although so many have been involved, the "big four" who have worked incessantly to preserve the area's history are the late John Stadnik, MaryAnn Goodlett-Taylor and Yvonne and Frank Shonberger. Just saying "thank you" is not enough, and to commemorate them and their great work in preserving history and communicating the importance of that history to the entire tri-city area, I warmly and lovingly dedicate this book to John (posthumously), MaryAnn, Yvonne and Frank with my—and the entire community's—unending thanks.

Contents

Acknowledgements

It is always a pleasure to extend thanks to those who have done so much to see to it that the plethora of photographs and information needed to make a book such as this successful are properly noted, and it is, therefore, with great gratitude that I recognize the following:

From Hialeah, Mayor Julio Robaina, who supported this project from the very beginning; Mayor Robaina's chief of staff, David Concepcion, who helped to smooth the way so many times; Lisa S. Espinosa, the city's Communications and Special Events Department supervisor, who was always ready to help; Elvis Santana, communications, marketing and media coordinator, who provided "tons" of material and information and was always "there" with photos and information; police department Lieutenant John Wall, who so kindly delivered several fine Hialeah Police Department photos; Alex Fuentes, the driving force behind the "Save Hialeah Park" group, who furnished much valuable information on Mr. Bright and the racetrack; Mercy and Raul Dominguez, who so kindly opened their home to me and shared immense amounts of information on early (and later) Hialeah; and Maricarmen Lopez, my former student (who is still in college!) and now the mayor's office receptionist, who was so helpful in introducing me to, among others, David Concepcion;

From Miami Springs, Mayor Billy Bain, who, like Mayor Robaina, was totally supportive; Vice-mayor Bob Best, who smoothed the way with various departments; City Manager James R. Borgmann, who came through so marvelously with photos of the mayor, commission, chief of police and other police views; Maryann Goodlett-Taylor, whose help and assistance, always proffered with a warm smile, cannot be quantified simply with a "thank you"; our friends Marian and her late husband Rod Zamotin, who were "with us" from the beginning; our longtime friends, Maria and Lloyd Mitchell, who were never too busy to help with information and statistics; Graciela Vazquez of the police department, who provided information on the department; the Glenn H. Curtiss Museum in his birthplace of Hammondsport, New York, who provided not only a copy of the Opa Locka booklet that was the catalogue of a University of Miami exhibition on the architecture of the city, but also six fine photographs of Mr. Curtiss and his accomplishments, including the Aerocar.

From Opa Locka, David Y. Smith and Valerie Caracappa graciously provided several Speedway photos, while Antolin G. Carbonell, R.A., was immensely helpful regarding the history of aviation in Opa Locka, his opus study being the preeminent authority on and about the topic; and friend Blair Conner provided much information on and about the Opa Locka Zoo.

From Virginia Gardens, Village Clerk Maritza Fernandez, the village's two administrative assistants Haydee Lopez and Carmen Spelorzi and Lieutenant Curtis G. Hodges were extremely helpful in providing maps and historical information, and from Hialeah Gardens, City Clerk Mari Joffee and administrative assistant Mirena Diaz were both marvelously helpful with information and photographs. To all of the above, as well as those who may not be named, but who certainly assisted and encouraged us, my warmest thanks and good wishes.

Introduction

The story of the Curtiss-Bright cities is an incredible, fascinating, totally unbelievable story! Except that it is true.

The Seminole interpretation of Hialeah's name, "High Prairie," evokes a picture of the grassy plains used by the native Indians who came from the Everglades to dock their canoes and display their wares for Miami's newcomers and tourists. That "high prairie" caught the eyes of pioneer aviator Glenn Curtiss (May 21, 1878–July 23, 1930) and Missouri cattleman James H. Bright (1866–January 5, 1959), who as early as 1909 saw its great potential.

In the early Roaring Twenties, Hialeah was considered a party city and entertainment was plentiful. Sporting activities included jai alai and greyhound racing, while the cinema included silent movies such as D.W. Griffith's "The White Rose," which was made at the Miami Movie Studios located in Hialeah. Although the four catastrophic events of 1926, culminating with the September 17–18 hurricane, brought an end to the great Florida boom that essentially began with the ending of World War I, it could not quench the spirit of those who knew what Hialeah could be.

In the years since its incorporation in 1925, many historical events and people have been linked with the city. The opening of Hialeah Park (which was nicknamed the Grande Dame) in 1925 as a horse track following its several years as a greyhound track, received more coverage in the Miami media than any other sporting event in the history of Miami up to that time. Since then there have been countless thoroughbred racing firsts and historical events at the world famous 220-acre park. It opened as one of the country's grandest thoroughbred horse racing parks with its majestic Mediterranean-style architecture and was considered the "Jewel of Hialeah" at the time, although, as this is being written, attempts and efforts are underway to save the now mostly abandoned park.

Across the river from Hialeah, Mr. Curtiss planned a Pueblo Indian–themed town, which, according to historian Hazel Streun, was to be a residential community set aside for gracious living. In 1922, Country Club Estates, as the town was originally called, was surveyed and laid out, although there was, initially, nothing on the site of what would become Miami Springs except a riding stable. Curtiss, who believed in putting his money where his mouth was, built his first house in the area in the Deer Park section of Hialeah, but in 1925, he moved to his newer and larger home in Country Club Estates, giving away tracts of land to those who would build homes immediately.

On August 23, 1926, Country Club Estates was incorporated as a town, and on April 15, 1930, the voters of that community changed its name to Miami Springs. With sixty registered voters at the time, thirty-three voted for the change with twenty-seven against.

To no small extent, since the 1930s Miami Springs has been home to innumerable transportation employees, both railroad and airline. The Florida East Coast Railway's Hialeah Yard is located just across the canal on the west side of the city, and airline employees appreciate the city's proximity to Miami International Airport just across Thirty-sixth Street to the south.

Of the three major cities that comprise this tome, one—Opa Locka—built by Curtiss with an Arabian nights theme, has sadly and unhappily fallen on hard times. Many of the original buildings either have been demolished or are uninhabitable, with too many of the current and extant buildings comprising substandard housing.

Opa Locka began life with the Indian name *Opatishawockalocka* as part of the 120,000-acre Curtiss-Bright Ranch and Dairy Farm. Curtiss, though, planned to shorten the name, and the first plat of the area, dated 1926, does show it as Opa Locka. According to *A Dream of Araby*, the marvelously researched history of Opa Locka written by the late Frank S. Fitzgerald-Bush and published in 1976, Curtiss formed the Opa Locka Development Company on December 11, 1925, with construction beginning in 1926. The municipal charter was dated May 14, 1926.

The city was planned, as noted above, with an Arabian nights theme, and the municipal building, the Seaboard Railway station and numerous other buildings fit that concept. Many of the streets bear names indicative of the theme, including Sharazad and Ali Baba Avenues, but even with that fanciful plan, the city never became what Curtiss had planned it to be, likely due in no small part to his much too early death.

Although not built by Curtiss or Bright, two other cities are part of the mosaic in this volume, namely Virginia Gardens and Hialeah Gardens, the former being carved out of a portion of Miami Springs fronting on Northwest Thirty-sixth Street on the south and Lafayette Drive on the north, from Northwest Fifty-seventh Avenue (Curtiss Parkway) on the east to Northwest Sixty-sixth Avenue and the Ludlum Canal on the west. Virginia Gardens was incorporated in 1947 and celebrated its sixtieth anniversary in 2007.

Hialeah Gardens, which extends northwest from Hialeah along and adjacent to U.S. 27 (Okeechobee Road), was incorporated by twenty-six voters in 1948. Its sixtieth anniversary year is 2008. With approximately twenty thousand people within its two and a half square miles, Hialeah Gardens is one of Miami–Dade County's most densely populated cities and is recognized as such with its own branch of the Miami–Dade Public Library System.

One

Glenn H. Curtiss and James H. Bright

U nlike many—if not most—of Dade County's cities, which can be identified with one name or one person, it took two farsighted visionaries to build the three major cities that are presented in this book. One of them was one of America's greatest and most famous aviation pioneers; the other, a man who had made his early fortune farming in Missouri and first came to south Florida in 1901. Fate—and like interests—would, thankfully for the cities that they would found, bring them together.

Glenn Hammond Curtiss was born in 1878 in Hammondsport, New York, to Frank Richmond Curtiss and Lua Andrews. Curtiss married Lena Pearl Neff, daughter of Guy L. Neff, in Logansport, Indiana, on March 7, 1898, and began his career as a bicycle racer, Western Union bicycle messenger and bicycle shop owner. He developed an interest in motorcycles when internal combustion engines became more available and began manufacturing motor bicycles with his own single-cylinder internal combustion engines, the first one having a tomato can for a carburetor! In 1903, he set a world speed record by averaging 64 mph (103 km/h) for one mile (1.6 km). In 1907 he set a new record of 136.36 mph (219.31 km/h)—without brakes!—on a 40-horsepower V8-powered motorcycle of his own design. At that time, he was America's number one maker of high-performance motorcycles.

Beginning just before World War I, he built sea- and land-based planes of his own design for the allies, and after the war, though purportedly "retired," he remained a technical advisor to the airplane manufacturing company that bore his name. Sometime following the war—the date is believed to be 1919—he ventured into south Florida where he bought his first piece of property on Northwest South River Drive in Miami, donating it to the U.S. Marine Corps. The corps utilized the property as their first U. S. base dedicated to aviation. Though the Marines soon outgrew the facility, the barracks building remained intact on the site for many years after the Marines had moved on to other bases, including the Opa Locka Marine Air Station.

In 1920, supposedly still in retirement, Curtiss purchased land from his friend and soon-to-be partner James H. Bright, and together they envisioned a town that would cater to winter visitors. Joining forces they formed the Curtiss-Bright Company (which had previously been the Curtiss-Bright Ranch Company), and with that partnership, the three main cities that compose the largest part of this book began to move from the partners' fertile imaginations to reality.

According to Hazel Streun in her privately printed *Beautiful Miami Springs*, Hialeah seemed to "just grow," and with the increasing population, a small business district began to develop at or near what is today's Hialeah Drive (Northwest Fifty-fourth Street in Miami) and Okeechobee Road. In 1925 Hialeah was incorporated, Mr. Bright personally laying out the city and paying for the streetlights, sidewalks and coral rock streets.

Across the river from Hialeah, Mr. Curtiss began to lay out Country Club Estates, later to become Miami Springs. Curtiss and Bright, so the story goes, stood on the canal bank on the Country Club Estates side of the Miami River Canal (technically, the canal is an extension of the Miami River and is referred to by some as the Miami River and by others as the Miami Canal) and visualized the town site of what would later become Miami Springs.

Curtiss was a quiet, almost taciturn man. He was kind and courteous, but unless one planned on conveying important ideas to him, conversation seemed to be fruitless. He was, in retrospect, so busy thinking of his next move that he just did not have time for small talk. Unfortunately, the Depression, coupled with his death in 1930 at the age of fifty-two, ended his participation in the partnership, and he was never able to complete his plans for Opa Locka.

Mr. Bright was born in 1866, most likely in Missouri, and though in his early fifties when he entered into the wonderful partnership with Glenn Curtiss, he would survive the great aviator by almost twenty-nine years, dying on January 5, 1959. He remained a director of Hialeah Race Track until his death.

In 1909, Bright planted three hundred acres of his south Florida property with para-grass clippings brought from Cuba, which would develop into rich grazing land for his cattle, and in 1911 he introduced the Brahman bull to the state. Its thick hide and imperviousness to heat made it an ideal breed of cattle for the Sunshine State. In 1916, Bright first met Curtiss, and in 1923 the pair incorporated the town of Hialeah, with thirteen square miles stretching north from the Miami River Canal.

Bright's home is still extant and remains in the Deer Park section of Hialeah, a beautiful neighborhood of quiet streets and well-tended houses. Incredibly foresighted, Bright gave the City of Miami seven miles of right of way from Miami to Hialeah and land at West Seventh Street and Okeechobee Road for a water pumping station, used to tap the Biscayne Aquifer and provide the area with clean, fresh water. But perhaps Mr. Bright's greatest interest was education (knowing that families would move to his and Curtiss's communities if good schools were available close by), and in 1923 he loaned the Dade County School Board $10,000 to build the South Hialeah Elementary School, telling them that, if it was not completely filled with pupils in two years, he would present the building to them as a gift. He did not need to, as the school, which opened in 1924, had every seat filled by 1926!

Both men had Miami–Dade County public schools named after them. The Glenn Curtiss Elementary School, which was in Miami Springs, was later turned into administrative offices by the school board, but James H. Bright Elementary School is thriving and prospering in Hialeah today.

Suffice to say, the legacy of these two inestimable men will live ever and always, as the cities they created stand as monuments to their foresight, determination and indomitable will.

Glenn Hammond Curtiss, circa 1907, at the age of twenty-nine. He was already involved with aviation, although he was still building motorbikes when this photograph was made. *Courtesy Glenn H. Curtiss Museum.*

Taken just a year before his untimely death in 1930, Glenn Curtiss was a world-renowned figure for his aviation exploits and, of course, had become part and parcel of south Florida's history and lore. *Courtesy Glenn H. Curtiss Museum.*

On June 9, 1930, to honor Curtiss for his exploits, both in aviation and as a Miami-area developer, the then four-year-old University of Miami presented him with an honorary Doctor of Science degree. Founding UM President Bowman Foster Ashe, at left, presents Curtiss with his degree while Dr. O.J. Selplein, right, places the hood on Curtiss's shoulders. *Courtesy Glenn H. Curtiss Museum, via the University of Miami collection.*

Curtiss's first home in south Florida was built in the Deer Park section of Hialeah. After Curtiss moved across the river/canal to Country Club Estates (Miami Springs), the home shown here became the Philbrick Funeral Home.

The Glenn Curtiss Mansion was built by Curtiss at 500 Deer Run and was his Florida residence until his death in 1930. Shown here in 1933 or '34, the photo was taken by Hiram Owen Goodlett. *Courtesy Miami Springs Historical Museum.*

The Curtiss-Bright Ranch's dairy is shown here. Comprising 120,000 acres, the exact location of the dairy is, today, impossible to divine, the majority of the records having been lost or destroyed throughout the ensuing years. By the automobiles, however, it can be determined that this view was made in the very early 1920s.

James H. Bright's Hialeah home. A believer in the area's future, Bright settled in what would eventually become Miami–Dade County's second or third largest city when it was nothing but open prairie.

Taken sometime after Curtiss's death, this one of a kind 1930s photograph was made at the Curtiss mansion and shows, in the front row, from left to right, Mingy Michaels, Mrs. Curtiss's mother, Mrs. Neff, Mrs. Curtiss Wheeler and Mrs. Carl Adams. Behind them are, from left to right, Glenn Curtiss Jr., Sayre Wheeler, Florence Illig, Carl Adams, unknown and M. Michaels. *Photograph donated to the Miami Springs Historical Museum by Mable Huffman and used courtesy of the museum.*

In 1946, Evelyn Marik Shull, second from right, and Mrs. Marik (first name unknown), second from left, were joined by three friends from Cleveland for a photograph in front of the entrance to the Curtiss Mansion. Notice the sign over the entranceway—"Dar-err-aha" or "house of happiness." *Photograph donated to the Miami Springs Historical Museum by Evelyn Marik Shull and used courtesy of the museum.*

In 1926 or '27, J.A. Michaels (shown center) lived in the first house in what would become Miami Springs. Although taken on Key Biscayne (the island that is now a city reached by the Rickenbacker Causeway) sometime in the 1960s, this photograph shows several contemporaries of Curtiss and Bright. *From left:* Mrs. Michaels, unknown, Mr. Michaels, Mrs. G. Carl Adams and Florence Illig. Several of the people shown here are also in the 1930s photograph shown opposite. *Photograph donated to the Miami Springs Historical Museum by Mabel Huffman and used courtesy of the museum.*

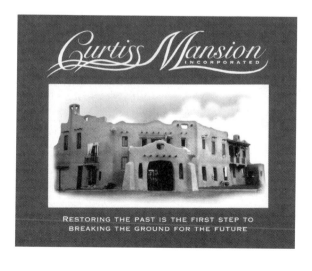

It is the great hope of many of the people of Miami Springs that, in time, they will be able to restore the Curtiss Mansion, which has been severely damaged by hurricanes and fire, and to that end, the group Curtiss Mansion Inc. (www.curtissmansion.org) has formed. To properly memorialize the life and times of one of south Florida's greatest and most revered pioneers, the long-term goal of the organization is to rebuild the house and restore the grounds so that the mansion can once again be a gathering spot for those interested in the glorious history of the Curtiss-Bright cities.

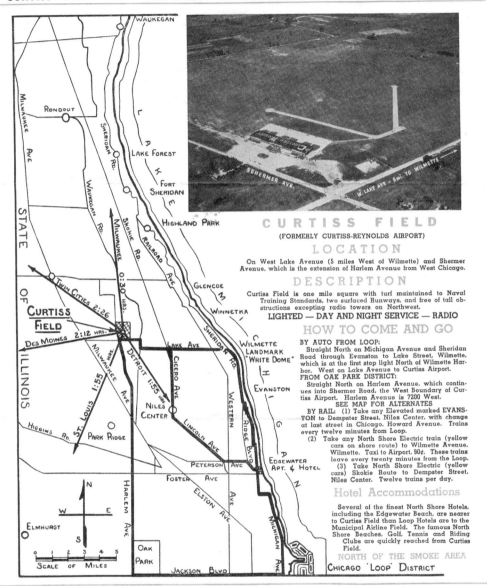

Glenn Curtiss was to early aviation what Henry Ford was to automobiles, excluding the blatant and hateful anti-Semitism that Ford was known for. This, the back of a piece of Curtiss Field letterhead, shows the airport and its location north of Chicago and west of Wilmette. The photo of the airport is especially striking, as the intersection shown—Schermer Avenue and West Lake Avenue five miles west of Wilmette, Illinois—is totally unrecognizable today.

Curtiss was an early believer not only in aviation but also in using water for takeoffs and landings. To a great extent it was he who developed the flying boat, later known as the seaplane. The first commercial airline in America was the St. Petersburg–Tampa Airboat Line (much to the shock of those who thought it was Western Airlines!), which was operated for twenty-eight days beginning on January 1, 1914, by Tony Benoist, who owned the flying boat. Benoist's pilot, Tony Jannus, would later be killed in World War I. Jannus's flight plan took him across Tampa Bay and cut several hours off the then lengthy rail trip around the top of the bay via Clearwater and Oldsmar, but he was only able to carry one passenger at a time, therefore the economics of the early service doomed it. Curtiss had begun experimenting with the flying boats in Tampa Bay as early as 1912, and one of his creations is shown here taxiing near St. Petersburg that same year.

At the boarding site in St. Petersburg in 1914, this incredible close-up of a Curtiss flying boat shows owner Tony Benoist, at left, and pilot Tony Jannus, right.

Glenn Curtiss, besides being a motorcycle and aviation enthusiast and pioneer, was a man of unlimited mechanical talents, and sometime in the 1920s he introduced one of America's first travel trailers, the Curtiss Aerocar, which he manufactured in Opa Locka, with sales offices in Coral Gables and at 535 Fifth Avenue in New York City. The Aerocar was nothing if not revolutionary and Curtiss's pride in his creation is evident here. Standing in front of his Miami Springs home in 1929, he is holding the door open inviting the viewer to inspect the Aerocar built for Merle D. Graves of Pittsfield, Massachusetts.

Especially significant, this photograph of the Curtiss Aerocar built for J.A. Seitz of Syracuse, New York, was taken in front of the then quite new Opa Locka City Hall, the city itself a creation of Mr. Curtiss. (It may have been the 119th Aerocar built, according to printing at bottom right of photo.) While the identities of the two men standing by the door are unknown, the fellow at right may be the well-known Aerocar mechanic J.A. "Jake" Honeysnork. *Both photographs courtesy of the Glenn H. Curtiss Museum.*

Two

Hialeah, the City

What a story! What an incredible, exciting story!

The location of today's Hialeah (Hi-a-le-ah in its early days!) was the same as the Seminole Indian village named *Hiyakpohilli*, or, reputedly, "pretty prairie," in the Seminole-Creek tongue.

By 1909, James H. Bright had settled in the area, and having purchased fourteen thousand acres of Everglades land (no national park in those days!), he had initiated his dairy farm, populating the pastures with his herd of cows. In 1917, Glenn Curtiss and another notable figure in Hialeah's history, Bob Millard, had begun to build a town on the banks of the Miami Canal, sometimes referred to as the Miami River Canal. By late 1920 the Curtiss-Bright Ranch, then the largest dairy, poultry yard and farm in Dade County, had moved farther north so that, in January of 1921, the partners could prepare the first plat of what would become a city. That plat covered a relatively small area of twenty-six blocks, with streets numbered First through Ninth and avenues with such delightful sounding names as Eucalyptus, Seminole, Chi-lock-o, Palm and Opa Locka.

The Seminoles living in the area were treated warmly and with respect by the early white residents, Mr. Bright leading the way when he said, "The Seminoles are the greatest race of people in the country, the most honorable people imaginable," and it was he who would, in many ways, work fervently to ensure that their rights were never ignored and that they were always welcome in Hialeah.

Hialeah was not an easy place to get to at that time, the only road leading to the town (later the city) being Northeast and Northwest Thirty-sixth Street, which led west to Okeechobee Road. In 1924, the Florida East Coast Railway (FEC)—as part of a grand plan to build a second mainline from New Smyrna Beach south through the Kissimmee Valley and around Lake Okeechobee, expecting eventually to come south on a right of way that is today's U.S. 27 from South Bay to Hialeah—built a line westward from its main tracks at today's Northeast Seventy-first Street in Miami to the racetrack with a station at that point. The railroad then crossed the canal and entered a large field that it would later convert to the railway's Hialeah Yard.

Excitement was in the air, as Hialeah had its railroad connection, and for a good few years from the late 1920s until the 1940s the FEC would operate Hialeah Park race train specials from both West Palm Beach and Miami. In 1926 the Seaboard Railway's line to Miami, passing through both Opa Locka and Hialeah (with stations being built to serve both cities) was opened, and the area was then served by mainline passenger trains.

Hialeah Park Race Track opened on January 15, 1925, with almost 18,000 people on hand for that event. On September 10, 1925, Hialeah, already boasting over 1,500 residents, was incorporated. By that date, twelve thousand lots and parcels of land had changed hands, and Curtiss-Bright's sales were more than $2,800,000. With the 1925 incorporation, and on the recommendation of Mr. Bright, Florida Governor John W. Martin appointed Jack P. Grethen as the city's first mayor. The first council election was held on September 10, 1929, and an incredible 829 out of 967 registered voters cast ballots that day, electing Grethen as their mayor for another term.

As with the rest of south Florida, the four terrible events of 1926, beginning with the capsizing of the four-masted schooner *Prinz Valdemar* at the mouth of the turning basin of Miami's harbor in early January and culminating with the vicious September 17–18 hurricane, would put a damper on growth in the area for many years to come. In fact, the events would prove to be the harbinger of the Great Depression that would begin in 1929, overwhelming the rest of the country and much of the world. However, Hialeah may have been down, but it was certainly not out! The track continued to draw record crowds through the late 1920s and even during the height of the Depression, as people poured in by car and train to enjoy a day's outing at America's most magnificent thoroughbred racing establishment.

In 1924, a young man by the name of Henry Milander came to Hialeah to work for a retail merchant and never looked back. A lover of politics, he watched the process with growing interest, and in 1943 he was elected mayor, serving one two-year term. Reelected in 1947 he would serve as mayor and Hialeah's voice until his retirement in 1972. Milander was succeeded by Dale Bennett, but "the times, they were a-changin," and in 1977 Raul Martinez was elected to the council.

Martinez's name has been identified with Hialeah in much the same manner as Milander's had been, as the crusader and spokesman for a great city. Elected mayor in 1981, Martinez served in that capacity until his retirement from Hialeah politics in 2005. On November 15 of the same year, a handsome young man, a veteran president of the city council (having served for five years) was elected mayor with 60 percent of the vote. Julio Robaina, only forty at the time he became mayor, has already made his mark on the city he loves, and it will be Robaina and his colleagues and associates who will lead Hialeah to a new level of greatness. They have already proven their willingness to listen to the citizenry and make changes as necessary, even if that means "shaking up" the so-called establishment. Julio Robaina was elected at precisely the right moment in time and will, unquestionably, be the man of the hour for Hialeah and its future.

Two views of Jack Tigertail (or Chief Willy Willy) show both ways of getting to Hi-a-le-ah in the early 1920s. One could come up the Miami River and swing into the Miami River Canal, using, among other boats, the *Biscayne*, which stopped at the entrance to Hialeah, or by road, take the long drive out today's Thirty-sixth Street and then turn northwest on Okeechobee Road, today's U.S. 27. In either case, the chief awaited all visitors, pointing to the east to show them where the Hi-a-le-ah welcome (and land sales) center was. *Photographs purchased from Pat Powers.*

Hialeah was, from the beginning, filled with civic boosters, and the first charter meeting of the Optimist Club of Hialeah was held at the now long gone Bagdad Club on February 18, 1926. At least seventy-nine people can be counted in this marvelous panoramic view. *Courtesy City of Hialeah.*

This is the first known photograph of the Hialeah Police Department. Taken in January 1925, the panoramic was made in front of the Studio Building, which served as the first police station and temporary jail. The twenty-five-man force included four motorcycle officers. *Courtesy City of Hialeah.*

This incredible photograph was made circa 1925. Taken at the intersection of Hialeah Drive (today's Northwest Fifty-fourth Street in Miami) and Okeechobee Road, the photograph is significant because it shows, at far left, on the Miami Springs side of the Miami River/Canal, the First State Bank of Hialeah. At center left is the Pueblo Indian–style bridge tender's house. At center right is the real estate office building (which was also a drugstore) that housed the first Hialeah post office, with R.G. "Bob" Millard as the first postmaster. In the right foreground is a corner of the Seminole Lodge building. *Courtesy Miami Springs Historical Museum.*

Sometime in 1924 the Curtiss-Bright publicity people posed a group of Hialeah children for this marvelous promotional view, as all twelve of the little ladies have their left arms raised and pointing to the left, emulating the stances of Big Chief Potchentouchouss at Northeast Thirty-sixth Street and Second Avenue in Miami and Chief Willy Willy in Hialeah.

The Civic Center of Country Club Estates, Hialeah, Florida —A Curtiss-Bright Property

Mimicking Coral Gables founder George Merrick's penchant for making it appear as if life in that city was golden, Curtiss and Bright published at least two (and likely more) goldtone postcards, this being one of them. Featuring the civic center of Country Club Estates, Hialeah, Florida, the card carefully notes at lower right that the development is a Curtiss-Bright Property.

Another Chamberlain photographic work was this fine look at The Follies, a famed (at the time) dining and dancing spot. When this picture was made The Follies featured the Jimmy Hodges dining and dancing revue.

This photograph was taken and published by the famed Miami photographer J.N. Chamberlain sometime in the early '20s. Featuring the Seminole Inn (also known as the Seminole Lodge, the terms, apparently, used interchangeably), the photo was a popular Hialeah souvenir view.

Yet another of the Chamberlain photos of Hialeah is this look at the Community Temple, believed to be the city's first house of worship, and it was likely multidenominational so as to provide a place of worship for the numerous religions seeking at least a temporary home prior to building their own facilities.

Sometime in the late 1930s Miami Post Card Company made this image of Hialeah's then new city hall available to the public. The building had been outgrown by the early 1960s and the Raul Martinez City Hall building at 501 Palm Avenue is, today, the center of the city's municipal activities.

The hurricane of November 4, 1935, devastated both Coral Gables and Hialeah, and though not as vicious as the September 2, 1935 hurricane that destroyed the FEC Railway's Key West Extension, the November storm not only caused the termination of the Coral Gables streetcar system but also wreaked extensive damage on Hialeah. Shown here, two women try to salvage anything they can from the remains of their likely uninsured wooden home, their puppy sitting forlornly in front of the lady on the left.

Beginning in the late 1940s, Pete and Jean's Gifts of the Tropics was a must-see while traveling to or from the racetrack, the selection enormous and the warm greetings and personal service of Pete and Jean Adleman well worth the time it took to stop by. *Courtesy Miami Springs Historical Museum.*

This view, made from the Miami Springs side of the canal, still shows Hialeah's spelling with the hyphens. At left is the real estate office/drugstore/post office, and to the right is the Seminole Inn/Lodge. The chief is on the left, just out of the picture.

This stunning tropical home was built in Hialeah by famed bandleader Arthur Pryor after he was lured to the city by James Bright. With its open archways on the porch, the house was cooled in the summer by the sea breezes, which, prior to the overbuilding symptomatic of all of south Florida, acted as a refresher for the entire area. Though not identified in this photo, it is believed that the two men shown are Pryor and Bright.

Photographed by J.N. Chamberlain, this is the first unit of the Hialeah Public School, which served the lower grades. Hialeah's high schoolers had a choice between Miami Edison, Miami High or Miami Jackson, but would only be allowed to take a bus to Edison, the choice of either of the other two schools causing them to have to make their own transportation arrangements.

Opened in 1954, this is the main entrance of Hialeah High School, the home of the Thoroughbreds. *Courtesy Miami Springs Historical Museum.*

The rear entrance of the school was at 261 East Forty-seventh Street. Subsequent reconstructions have moved the main entrance to Forty-seventh Street. Today the school is one of Miami–Dade County's largest public high schools. *Courtesy Miami Springs Historical Museum.*

SEE
THE MUSEUM
AS YOU LEAVE
HIALEAH RACE
COURSE

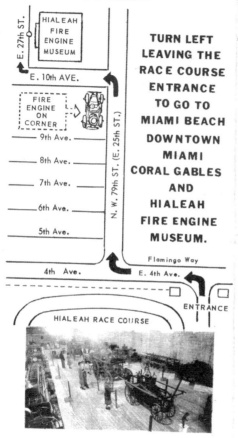

TURN LEFT LEAVING THE RACE COURSE ENTRANCE TO GO TO MIAMI BEACH DOWNTOWN MIAMI CORAL GABLES AND HIALEAH FIRE ENGINE MUSEUM.

HIALEAH FIRE ENGINE MUSEUM

E. 27th ST.

E. 10th AVE.

FIRE ENGINE ON CORNER

9th Ave.

8th Ave.

7th Ave.

6th Ave.

5th Ave.

N. W. 79th ST. (E. 25th ST.)

Flamingo Way

4th Ave.

E. 4th Ave.

ENTRANCE

HIALEAH RACE COURSE

Among Hialeah's greatest attractions, from the late 1940s until the late 1960s, was Vincent K. O'Meara's "Famous Hialeah Fire Engine Museum," now, regretfully, mostly forgotten except by Hialeah historians and researchers. O'Meara, a fireman for sixteen years, began collecting fire memorabilia at a young age and eventually owned thousands of artifacts and more than thirty engines. Unfortunately, as he aged, his pleas to the municipality and county to take over the museum and make it a public facility fell on deaf ears, and with his death the collection was dispersed throughout the country.

While Hialeah had several movie theatres, the Essex, at 439 Hialeah Drive, was always one of the great favorites.

On November 11, 1953, the city celebrated Armistice Day, commemorating the end of World War I and honoring all veterans. While their names have been lost in the mists of time, a group of American Legion members stands in front of Hialeah's war memorial in tribute to those who served.

Prior to their November 11, 1953 concert, the Hialeah Junior High School band poses proudly in front of the city's bandshell.

Hialeah–Miami Springs Bank's pedigree in and with the two communities goes back to its founding in 1925. Founded by James H. Bright, the bank went through several moves and incarnations. It is shown here, at 101 Hialeah Drive, in the early 1950s.

Shown on October 5, 1955, Hialeah Drive is undergoing a major repaving and improvement project. At left is the Hialeah–Miami Springs Bank, while on the right, just past the Pix Shoes store is the former Florida Cafeteria; the building, at 120 Hialeah Drive, is vacant and for rent.

A close-up of the cafeteria building on October 14, 1956, shows the business sign still in place above the door with a "For Rent" sign prominent in the window to the left of the front doors.

A marvelous aerial view, made on October 14, 1956, looks southeast above Okeechobee Road, the Miami River Canal to the right of that fabled drive. Across the canal, to the viewer's right, is Miami Springs; the two bridges, still in place today, connect Hialeah and Miami Springs.

On December 18, 1956, an unknown photographer snapped this photo of the intersection of East Third Avenue and Okeechobee Road. Note that there is one traffic light protecting the intersection.

The area of East Fourth Avenue and Okeechobee Road, looking east into Hialeah, is also shown on December 18, 1956. Like Third Avenue, the intersection is virtually unrecognizable today.

On May 29, 1957, Palm Avenue was relatively quiet, this photo likely made fairly early in the morning that day. On the right is Baker's Pharmacy and on the left is Palm Shoe Store and Murphy's paints. The author believes that this view looks south on Palm toward Okeechobee Road in the distance.

Prior to Hialeah's expansion to the north and West 49th Street (Northwest 103rd Street in Miami) becoming a major business street, complete with Westland Mall, most shopping was done in or near the downtown area, particularly on Hialeah Drive (Northwest 54th Street) and Palm Avenue, the latter the long north-south street that divides east and west Hialeah. Shown here in this 1959 view looking east on Hialeah Drive, Mary Meeskite walks along the street with Jackson's (a longtime, famous Miami-area retail store now long gone) and McCrory's across the street in the distance.

McCrory's was at 177 Hialeah Drive and was an important addition to Hialeah's commercial and retail trade when it opened. This November 18, 1955 photograph made shortly after that opening.

As did most drug and five-and-ten-cent stores, McCrory's boasted a lunch counter that was a popular gathering and meeting place. Mostly replaced by fast food restaurants, there are today only about four or five (if that many!) drugstores with lunch counters in the Greater Miami area, and the five-and-dime has been replaced by discount stores and "big-box" retailers.

On September 14, 1965, planning for the opening of a new Black Angus restaurant, partners Jack Silver, far left, and Herb Brodsky, far right, pose in front of the sign announcing the groundbreaking of the store in the Palm Springs Mile shopping area, at 885 West Forty-ninth Street. The four individuals between them are unknown.

Silver and Brodsky were great promoters and Black Angus was a successful multiunit chain for many years. When the new Hialeah store opened it included a pony ride for the children, which, of course, proved to be a major draw for families.

It has never been a problem finding a favorite restaurant in Hialeah, and from snacks and fast food to gourmet ethnic, the city contains them all. On July 30, 1959, one of the city's first Burger Kings is shown at 600 East Ninth Street. Hialeah High's Mike Marook is checking out the newest model cars as he walks by.

Thai House was at 715 East Ninth Street and the beautiful interior alone was worth the visit. The young couple is obviously enjoying their Thai delicacies, her order for the evening that wonderful Thai favorite, Pad Thai with shrimp.

Still in business in Hialeah, the Hitching Post was getting ready to open at 1866 East Fourth Avenue (now located at 445 East Okeechobee Road) on June 2, 1954. The new owners, shown in the rear of the store, are hard at work just days before the opening.

Hialeah Hospital has been a mainstay of the well-being and good health of the area's residents for more than half a century, having opened circa 1950. Several of the original buildings, shown here and now long gone, will bring back warm memories to those who served in or were patients at the hospital.

Hialeah's hospitality industry thrived for many years with a number of mom and pop motels doing an excellent business thanks to the racetrack and the truckers. While, today, several new chain motels close to the Palmetto Expressway are the favored spots, several of the inns built in the 1940s and '50s survive. The Hialeah Motel, at 505 Okeechobee Road, advertised itself as "air cooled," meaning, of course, that in order to get relief from the heat one opened the windows and turned on the fan!

Roy's Motel was at 1280 West Twenty-ninth Street. Though boasting kitchens and a private swimming pool, no mention was made of air conditioning!

The Vic and Betty Motel at 1300 Okeechobee Road advertised itself as being "one of the finest on the waterway," but, apparently, that finery came without air conditioning!

Hialeah is, today, Miami–Dade County's second largest city, and oh, how it has changed! Shown here, on October 27, 1961, is the intersection of West Twelfth Avenue and Okeechobee Road—totally unrecognizable today.

West Twelfth Avenue and Eighty-fourth Street on March 9, 1966, with its sign on the left advertising Palm Springs Lakes homes for from $15,500 to $29,400, is another incredible memory.

Perhaps one of the most unbelievable street scenes of all time in Hialeah is the at-grade crossing of West Forty-ninth Street and State Road 826 on August 22, 1961. Now, more than forty-five years later, that intersection is one of the most highly trafficked in the state, the 826, also known as the Palmetto Expressway, a twenty-four-hours-a-day, eight-lane traffic nightmare. This view, looking north on 826, shows the crossing with West Forty-ninth Street protected only by a flashing light.

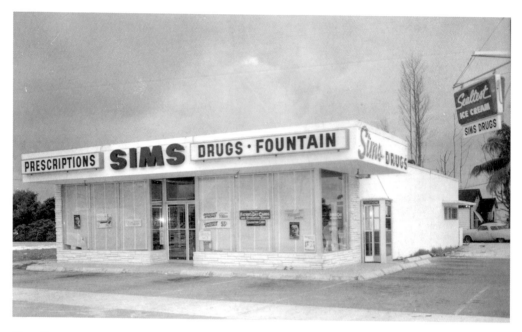

Sims Drugs was at 4090 East Eighth Avenue and was a neighborhood mainstay and gathering spot for years, complete with lunch counter and pharmacy. The building and its smiling druggists are shown here on April 29, 1959.

Hialeah was—and still is—a great place to grow up, but instead of video arcades and shopping malls, the families went to Rustic Roller Rink and enjoyed hours meeting, socializing and, of course, skating!

Always a commercial city, Hialeah was known for its local merchants and manufacturing. Hialeah Furniture Store, at 300 Palm Avenue, is shown on May 6, 1957, while the smiling crew of Kinney Shoe Store, at 26 Flamingo Plaza, was photographed on November 23, 1956. The televisions in the window of Palm TV and Appliance Sales and Service at 4165 Palm Avenue will certainly bring back thoughts of 1956, the storefront being photographed on September 24 of that year.

Today, Hialeah boasts several fine residential neighborhoods. Sometime in the early 1950s, though, with the Cold War at its height, Florida Sun Deck Homes Company, at 2019 East Fourth Avenue, publicized its "moderately priced, U.S. Department of Defense recommended solid concrete homes for protection against the atom bomb."

Ten years later, on November 19, 1963, the home of Joseph Pecci at 577 West Fifty-third Street has a completely different look, complete with its jalousie windows and open carport, and the wonderful terrazzo floors de rigeur in new Florida homes of the era.

On September 25, 1957, Hialeah Christian Church, at 441 East Twelfth Street, is seen basking in the Florida sunshine.

Immaculate Conception Catholic Church was dedicated on February 29, 1964. Located at 68 West Forty-fifth Place, Monsignor Dominic J. Barry was pastor at the time.

Shown at its "new" location at Palm Avenue and Seventeenth Street, the original fountain that welcomed visitors to Hialeah was moved intact so that the stunning new entrance to the city could be enlarged and a magnificent new fountain put in place. *Courtesy City of Hialeah.*

Located at Okeechobee Road, this is Hialeah's beautiful new entrance. Celebrating a city going through a marvelous renaissance, the new fountain is indicative of a fresh way of both thinking and doing business in Hialeah, which will only lead to a greater and brighter future for the city. *Courtesy City of Hialeah.*

Police Chief Rolando Bolanos, a thirty-four-year veteran in law enforcement, has been Hialeah's chief since 1987. Holder of a master's degree in public administration from Florida International University, the chief is a graduate of the FBI National Academy and a past president of the Dade County Association of Chiefs of Police. *Courtesy Hialeah Police Department.*

The Hialeah Police motorcycle unit and the K-9 unit, both shown here, are made up of highly trained and dedicated officers who give untold hours of their time to the service of their city. Hialeah's police department includes 371 sworn officers and 119 civilian employees. *Both photos courtesy Hialeah Police Department.*

Fighting the Hialeah Lumberyard fire at 4931 East Tenth Avenue on February 25, 1954, three of the fire department's "first in–last out" responders are shown hosing down the still smoldering embers of the massive blaze.

Under the direction of Chief Otto Drozd, Hialeah boasts one of the nation's finest fire departments. The city's superb fire/rescue equipment is exemplified by ladder truck seven, which is, like all of the department's equipment, magnificently and meticulously maintained. *Courtesy City of Hialeah.*

Under the direction of Mayor Henry Milander, who served first as councilman and then as mayor from 1947 until 1972, the city made enormous strides toward modernity. Milander is shown here, at center, examining a display of the city's sidewalk program on August 29, 1956.

Hialeah's stunningly beautiful new city hall, named for longtime Mayor Raul Martinez is a testament to the "new Hialeah." *Courtesy City of Hialeah.*

Two of the greatest and most recognizable names in Hialeah's equally glorious history stand together during a civic celebration. At left is current mayor Julio Robaina, while at right is the man he succeeded, longtime Hialeah booster and twenty-four-year mayor, Raul Martinez. *Courtesy City of Hialeah.*

He is, unquestionably and with total certainty, the man who can, should and will lead Hialeah into a great and bold new future. His warm smile, engaging personality and belief in the city he loves and leads are evident in this view of Mayor Julio Robaina waving from the front seat of the city's completely restored first fire truck. Driving is Fire Chief Otto Drozd, while behind them are, from left, Councilman Jose Caragol, Councilwoman Vivian Casals-Munoz, Council President Esteban Bovo and State Representative Eddy Gonzalez, who represents the city's residents in Tallahassee. *Courtesy City of Hialeah.*

Three

Hialeah, the Racetrack and Park

R acing in Hialeah actually began not with horses but with dogs, for the first track in the area was a greyhound racing track built at Palm Avenue and Twenty-first Street. According to Alex Fuentes, founder of Citizens to Save Hialeah Park, the first races were held there in 1922. Lasting only until the 1926 hurricane destroyed the track, its venue was graced on a fairly regular basis by such luminaries of the time as the great heavyweight boxing champion Jack Dempsey. According to the April 26, 1974 issue of the *Hialeah–Miami Springs Home News*, in 1931 the property was purchased by the City of Hialeah to provide additional stable space for the thoroughbred track.

The story of Hialeah Park, at one time the most beautiful horse racing track in America, if not the world, actually began in late 1923, when Bright provided the land for a racing facility, giving Buffalo, New York investor Joseph Smoot 160 acres for ten dollars to encourage Smoot to build what would become Hialeah Park and the Miami Jockey Club. On January 25, 1925, the Jockey Club launched Hialeah's racetrack into prominence with close to eighteen thousand people present for the first day of racing. Although gambling was then illegal in Florida, most communities looked the other way, and the track flourished even though parimutuels did not become legal until 1931.

The facility was severely damaged by the 1926 hurricane, but was soon rebuilt to become the iconic landmark much beloved by racing aficionados throughout America. In 1930 the park was sold to wealthy Philadelphia horseman Joseph E. Widener. With renowned Kentucky horseman and Palm Beach casino operator Colonel Edward R. Bradley as an investor, Widener hired architect Lester W. Geisler to design a completely new grandstand and Renaissance Revival clubhouse facilities, along with landscaped gardens of native flora and fauna and a lake in the infield that Widener stocked with flamingos, which became the nationally recognized symbol of the track. Hailed as one of the most beautiful racetracks in the world, Hialeah Park officially reopened on January 14, 1932. It became so famous for its flocks of flamingos that were originally imported from Cuba that it was officially designated a sanctuary for the American flamingo by the Audubon Society.

With various changes in ownership and a changing demographic, as well as interest in parimutuels decreasing with the emergence of Florida's Indian casinos complete with slot machines, Hialeah's era as the grande dame of Florida's horse racing tracks was at an end, and on one of the saddest days in the history of sports or recreation in Florida, owner John Brunetti closed the park to the public in 2001. The filly Cheeky Miss won the last race ever run at Hialeah on May 22, 2001, but its facilities remain intact except for the stables, which were demolished in early 2007.

Fortunately, the story may yet have a happy ending for a group of dedicated sports people, racing historians and Hialeah history buffs have banded together under the name "Save Hialeah Park" (www.savehialeahpark.com) to both raise money and convince the city fathers—and the region's citizens—that the magnificent property, with its incredible history, must be saved for posterity.

Two extremely rare views of dog racing at Hialeah. The first captures the greyhounds being walked around the track prior to being placed in the starting gate, circa 1923–24, and the second, the start itself, the dogs just breaking away from the hand-operated gate in 1924.

The fabled "Manassas Mauler," Jack Dempsey, loved south Florida, his trips to the area beginning as early as 1923 or '24. Besides purchasing a hotel on Miami Beach, he loved "the dogs" and was a frequent winter visitor to the Hialeah greyhound track. He is shown here holding a trophy for one of the races, standing at far left with hat in hand, and in the other view, he is enjoying a ride on the "bucking Ford" that, apparently, was one of the track's draws.

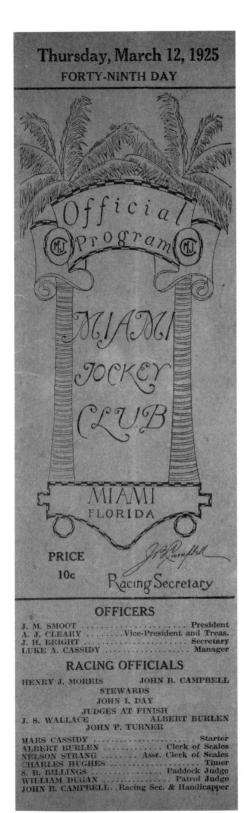

Thursday, March 12, 1925
FORTY-NINTH DAY

Official Program

MIAMI JOCKEY CLUB

MIAMI
FLORIDA

PRICE
10c

Racing Secretary

OFFICERS
J. M. SMOOT .... President
A. J. CLEARY .... Vice-President and Treas.
J. H. BRIGHT .... Secretary
LUKE A. CASSIDY .... Manager

RACING OFFICIALS
HENRY J. MORRIS   JOHN B. CAMPBELL
STEWARDS
JOHN I. DAY
JUDGES AT FINISH
J. S. WALLACE   ALBERT BURLEN
JOHN P. TURNER

MARS CASSIDY .... Starter
ALBERT BURLEN .... Clerk of Scales
NELSON STRANG .... Asst. Clerk of Scales
CHARLES HUGHES .... Timer
S. B. BILLINGS .... Paddock Judge
WILLIAM DUGAN .... Patrol Judge
JOHN B. CAMPBELL. .Racing Sec. & Handicapper

One of the rarest pieces of Hialeah Park horse racing memorabilia, the program for the forty-ninth day of racing during the first (1925) season is shown here. Issued on Thursday, March 12, 1925, J.M. Smoot is shown as president and J.H. Bright as secretary. To Miami memorabilia collectors, Hialeah historians and racing fans, the value of this piece is inestimable.

An early view of the infield in front of the clubhouse, this photograph was likely taken in the late 1930s, the park even then renowned for its beauty.

Although undated, we know from the cars on the right side of this image that this view was taken in the early to mid-1930s. Showing the royal palm esplanade toward the clubhouse, we are treated to a glimpse of the beauty visitors saw when they came to the track.

The November 4, 1935 hurricane, while not nearly as brutal as the September 2 storm, which destroyed forty miles of the FEC Railway's Key West Extension and literally turned over the rescue train sent to bring the veterans back from the work camp at Matecumbe Key, was extreme in its intensity, and the park suffered terribly. This view, taken several days following the storm, shows the damage inflicted on the palms by the hurricane.

Part of any visit to the park included visiting the flamingos, the original flock imported from Cuba. In this scene, the adult birds are attending to their young, a white flamingo chick standing in the foreground.

For sixty years no visit to Miami was or would have been complete without a visit to America's most magnificent racetrack. The beauty of the park is totally evident in this incredible 1930s view, the infield packed with visitors on a sunny south Florida winter day.

What a picture! Probably made in the early 1930s, the track is surrounded by...nothing! Mayor Robaina, Hialeah's biggest booster, is currently working ardently to have the track's racing dates restored and has stated that he will support slot machines for Miami–Dade County parimutuels (Broward already has them) provided that racing is again allowed at Hialeah. That insightful move would, indeed, create several thousand jobs for the city and put tens of millions of dollars into its economy.

Another aerial view, this one made on January 30, 1952, shows the stables behind (west of) the clubhouse, but blocks of land are still unoccupied to the west of Palm Avenue—the street behind (or in front of!) the stables.

DC-137 Champion Citation at Hialeah Race Course, Miami, Fla.

Among Hialeah's greatest thoroughbreds was the incomparable Citation, shown here with famed jockey Willie Shoemaker "up." The horse is commemorated by a statue at the park.

Two great races highlighted Hialeah's season each year: the Widener and the Flamingo Stakes. Though the year is unknown, this is the finish of that year's $50,000-Widener. Widener day and Flamingo Stakes day were the track's busiest days, with crowds in the multithousands and the handle, even then, in the multimillions.

A favorite with visitors to the park, both on- and off-season, was the tram, which took them around the grounds, allowing them to enjoy the stunning beauty of the park and its surroundings. A huge banyan tree is in the background.

Keeping track of the ever-changing odds was the Totalizer Board, which automatically registered bets and showed the odds as they were updated on all entries for each race. This photograph was made by revered longtime Miami photographer Gleason Waite Romer.

Sometime in the early 1970s, the park's ownership published this six-by-nine-inch booklet detailing the features of the racetrack and presenting the innumerable beautiful vistas available to racing aficionados and other visitors. With the great and ongoing work of the Save Hialeah Park group, there is no question that the park cannot only be saved but also that it can be restored to its former magnificence.

Four

Miami Springs

With an almost lyrical name, the very words "Miami Springs" harken back to ethereal thoughts and memories. The city, born as Country Club Estates, is actually built over a series of deep wells that supply millions of gallons daily to the Greater Miami community, the result of the knowledge and caring of Glenn Curtiss, who was aware of the existence of said wells.

Once Hialeah's lots and property had been sold, Curtiss began the sale of land in what was called, beginning in 1922, Country Club Estates. The lots there went for the startlingly high price (for the time) of $1,200 each, compared to some of the same sized lots selling in Hialeah for $75 each. When Curtiss began the sale of the lots, there was, according to Hazel Streun, only one building on the west/south side of the canal—a riding stable. Miami Springs' foremost historian, Maryann Goodlett-Taylor, remembers the stable being located across from what would become the site of the Methodist Church, which would place it close to the later property of the city's public works department.

To do the surveying, Curtiss brought in, among others, W.J. "Bill" Knox, Darrell Marple and Evan Gobat. Two of the engineers were Harry Howell and Dan Clune. Curtiss, with an almost eerie prescience, somehow knew that below the Estates was a major freshwater supply, and in drilling test bores, the water was discovered. Curtiss originally drilled fifteen wells, and it was from those that much of Greater Miami's water originally came.

In 1923, with the beginnings of the great Florida land boom under way, Curtiss sold 183 acres of his land south of the canal to the City of Miami for $90,000. The land would be used by Miami to build a golf course. When completed, and although owned by the City of Miami, the golf course was named the Miami Springs Golf Course. (On October 23, 1997, Miami Springs purchased the course from the City of Miami, floating a bond issue of $5 million to buy the property and to make needed improvements, allowing the city to finally take control of one of its greatest municipal assets.)

The first four homes in the Estates were built in a quadrangle, placed quite close together in order to take advantage of the single water pump available to the four property owners. According to Ralph Wakefield, in his 2001 history of Curtiss and the city, the four owners would take turns getting up early to prime the pump in the morning so that there was enough water each day for the four residences! Interestingly, one of the residents in the quadrangle of homes was Curtiss's mother, Mrs. Lua Curtiss!

J.A. Michael, who is mentioned several times in this volume, was the first resident of the Estates. Other houses were built, including Curtiss's home, and in 1925 Mr. Curtiss left Hialeah and moved into his new house at 500 Deer Run.

To increase the town's population, Curtiss gave away homesites to those who would agree to build a home immediately upon receipt of the land. Many of the grateful acceptors were former employees and pilots who had worked with or for him. Builder Francis Miller, the first mayor of the Estates, constructed no few of the original homes.

On August 23, 1926, Country Club Estates was incorporated as a town and a full slate of officers, from mayor to town marshal, was installed. Francis Miller served as the first mayor, and J.A. Michael was among the councilmen. R.H. Hall became town marshal. Less than four years later, on April 15, 1930, by a vote of 33 to 27, the voters changed the name of the town to Miami Springs, a name that has garnered national fame and attention as the home of several famous individuals, including football star Ted Hendricks and astronaut Ken Mattingly.

Not quite a month after the first council was sworn in, on September 17 and 18, a horrific hurricane ravaged the area, including Country Club Estates. Though the area was battered and bruised and land sales declined following the storm, Curtiss kept his word and completed the magnificent Hotel Country Club in the Pueblo Indian style that he so fancied. After some delays (construction had actually begun in 1925), the hotel was opened in 1929. Later that year, Dr. John Harvey Kellogg, founder of the Battle Creek Sanitarium in Michigan who was known as "the cornflakes king," visited south Florida. As fate would have it, he heard about Country Club Estates and upon arriving there was so enamored of it and the weather that he rented a home on the golf course adjoining Mr. Curtiss's house, and the two became fast friends. Even with the great Florida boom having ended and the area's economy in decline, Kellogg felt and believed that it would be a propitious move to open a southern branch of his famous sanitarium.

Curtiss, feeling that he had an opportunity to relieve himself of the enormous burden of operating a hotel at a time when the nation's worst depression was blanketing the nation, made Kellogg an offer he couldn't refuse: if Kellogg would promise to keep the hotel/sanitarium open for six months a year, Curtiss would turn it over to him for the princely sum of ONE dollar! In May 1930, the papers were signed and the hotel became Miami–Battle Creek Sanitarium, a name it retained for many years until being sold again and becoming Fair Havens Center, operating as it does today as an adult congregate living facility.

Tragically, the great Glenn Curtiss, at the comparatively young age of fifty-two, would die on July 23, 1930, from a pulmonary embolism following a routine appendectomy. Curtiss Parkway, one of Miami Springs' most important thoroughfares, bears his name and honors his memory.

Another place of great interest to locals in Country Club Estates was a zoo, located at Curtiss Square at the foot of South Poinciana. A map of Miami Springs, dated 1942, still shows the zoo in that location. Populated by all manner of fauna—including Bozo the gorilla, who was sold to John Ringling and became known as Gargantua—the zoo, which operated simultaneously with the Opa Locka Zoo, would close fairly early. The Opa Locka Zoo, also a Curtiss innovation used to draw tourists, later moved to North Miami, where it became known for its Galapagos tortoises and as the home of Captain Roman Proske and his trained tigers.

The need for a bank was not overlooked, either, and in January 1925, according to Hazel Streun, the First State Bank in Hialeah opened in the former Oleeta Lodge Building with Mr. Curtiss serving as president. The 1930 incorporation required a name change and the words "Miami Springs" were substituted for "Hialeah," the words "First State" being dropped in 1945. The bank was known as Miami Springs Bank until 1951, when it moved back across the canal to Hialeah, the name changing again to Hialeah–Miami Springs Bank.

In 1937, Miami Springs Elementary School opened, followed by Glenn Curtiss School in 1953. As noted previously the Curtiss School no longer carries that name, but Miami Springs is home to four fine public schools, including an elementary, middle and high school, which carry the Miami Springs name, and the fourth an elementary school named Springview.

When Miami Springs was incorporated in 1930 there were 60 registered voters. By 1940 the population had reached 898 and by 1953 there were 10,000 people living in the city. In the early 1950s, the city began annexation proceedings of a triangular-shaped area just northeast of the city that had been known as the Kent Estates and was also known as "the birds section" because most of the streets had been named after avians, including, among others, Oriole, Thrush, Bluebird, Redbird and Plover. The annexation, according to the April 26, 1974 thirtieth anniversary edition of *Hialeah–Miami Springs Home News*, was completed in 1955.

Miami Springs today is a vibrant 3.1-square-mile business and residential community of more than 13,700 people, governed by the city manager form of government and presided over by a five-person council, including current Mayor Billy Bain. City Manager James R. Borgmann, whose family moved to Miami Springs in 1958, oversees approximately 141 full-time and 68 part-time employees, including a police department with 43 sworn officers and 22 civilian employees. He attended Miami Springs Elementary, Miami Springs Junior High and was one of the first students to attend the new Miami Springs Senior High when it opened its doors in 1964. Borgmann was elected to the city council in 1985 and served on that body until 1993. In 1995 he became assistant city manager and in 2003 was named city manager.

One of Miami Springs' most beautiful and valuable assets is the golf course, which, as noted above, the city bought back from the City of Miami in 1997. Shown here sometime in the late 1930s, a group of duffers is working on their strokes on the putting green.

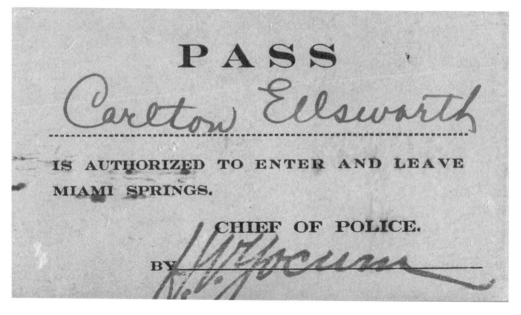

Apparently, at some point in its history, access to Miami Springs was restricted. It is possible that this pass was issued sometime early in World War II, but nobody associated with the city or the Miami Springs Historical Museum has any recollection of the card's use, the number issued or to whom it was issued. *Courtesy Miami Springs Historical Museum.*

The first town marshal of Miami Springs was Walter D. Kniffin, a retired military man. Kniffin, who had been an MP in the 107th Infantry in the 1920s, was the ideal person for the one-man office. *Photograph donated to the Miami Springs Historical Museum by Wally Clark and used courtesy of the museum.*

Among the early residents of Country Club Estates was Andrew "Andy" Heermance, shown here at far right during a lawn bowling event with friends, who, regretfully, are unknown. *Courtesy Miami Springs Historical Museum.*

Fortunately, the three young women in this photograph, taken in 1928 at Country Club Estates, are identified. *From left*: Elizabeth Lewis, Ruth Dunning and Clara Marik. *Photograph donated to the Miami Springs Historical Museum by Evelyn Marik Shull and used courtesy of the museum.*

The Hunting Lodge at 281 Glendale Drive. Built in 1924 by Mr. Curtiss for his personal use and later called Hialeah Shooting Park, the lodge served the town as its first elementary school (1926–33) and was known as Country Club Estates School, the smallest public school in Dade County. Beginning in 1933 it was used as a residence. In 1994 it was designated as a Miami Springs Historic Site. Taken sometime during the building's years as a school, a group of students and teachers are shown on the porch. *Courtesy Maryann Goodlett-Taylor collection.*

One of Miami Springs' true pioneers and early residents was Hiram Owen Goodlett, father of Maryann Goodlett-Taylor and Curtiss Estate chauffeur and gardener from 1933 until 1943. Hiram, shown near the pool of the estate with his friend, the harlequin Great Dane "Rex"—owned by Mrs. Lena Curtiss and her husband H. Sayre Wheeler—was, happily to report, a great favorite of the dog, who, obviously, one would not want to be disliked by! *Courtesy Maryann Goodlett—Taylor collection.*

In the first of two views of Stadnik's Miami Springs Drug Store, we can see "Oleeta-145" directly above the Coca-Cola sign in the front of the building. To the left of the drugstore, owned for many years by Miami Springs Historical Museum benefactor John Stadnik, is the long gone movie theater. It appears, from the design of the cars at left, that this photograph was made in the very late 1940s or possibly in 1950.

A similar view shows Stadnik's circa 1953, the Oleeta sign painted over and the building by then adorned with the Rexall Drug signs, of which Stadnik's was an agency for many years.

With the Curtiss-Bright administration building in the background, the first town of Miami Springs uniformed police squad stands proudly at attention, the town's motorcycle and police car behind them. *From left*: Hugh Frank, E.P. Lott, Walter Kniffin, L.K. Cropper and Hoyt Buxton. Because his winged-tire motorcycle emblem is visible on his left sleeve, it is evident that Officer Frank was the motorman. *Courtesy Miami Springs Historical Museum.*

Then as now, Miami Springs, a city of beautiful homes, boasts some of the largest lots and most elegant properties in Miami–Dade County. Shown at 141 Shadow Way in 1957 is the home of Hiram Goodlett, complete with an open carport. *Courtesy Miami Springs Historical Museum.*

Osceola Apartments/Hotel, later known as Azure Villas, was constructed in 1925 at what is now the southwest corner of Morningside and Glen Way. Shown here in 1984, the photograph was taken by Maryann Goodlett-Taylor. *Courtesy Miami Springs Historical Museum.*

This Maryann Goodlett-Taylor photograph shows another 1925 Springs home built by the Curtiss-Bright Company at 160 Sunset Way. Originally owned by H.K. Highhouse, the home, completely modernized on the inside, retains its charm. *Courtesy Miami Springs Historical Museum.*

Just prior to the Curtiss sale of the Country Club Hotel to Dr. Kellogg in May 1930, it was photographed by the Curtiss publicity people, possibly for the last time while still in Curtiss's ownership. The magnificence of the building is quite evident in this early 1930 view.

A side view of the center tower just after the Kellogg purchase. The building and property were extraordinary.

According to those who have seen this very rare postcard issued by Miami–Battle Creek Sanitarium shortly after Dr. Kellogg took it over, this marvelous look at the "Tropical Pool" shows the good doctor himself examining the flora in and around the pool.

Although many of the publicity views of the Country Club Hotel and the Miami–Battle Creek Sanitarium were very similar, it is interesting to note that this rarely seen shot of one of the guest bedrooms was made for the hotel, prior to Kellogg's ownership.

Shown in the mid-1930s, this view of the lobby looking toward the fireplace includes a glimpse of the front desk at right.

The hotel/sanitarium dining room was "the best place in town," and the food and service were always "the best." Ready to welcome guests, the dining room is adorned in its evening finery.

Another view of the lobby looking toward the fireplace is eerily reminiscent of the famous Pacific Electric Railway's Mount Lowe Inn on Mount Lowe above Pasadena in California. Though on opposite sides of the country, each hostelry had its ardent supporters.

The lounge room, complete with a guest library, was a favorite spot for those seeking the company of other guests or wishing to hear some impromptu piano playing. Drinks could also be ordered while one luxuriated in this beautiful room.

In a corner of the dining room, Julitta Ellsworth, longtime hotel fixture, Miami Springs resident and nurse, explains terminology on the menu to guests. Ellsworth was a multiyear employee of the Miami–Battle Creek Sanitarium, and Miami Springs historian Maryann Goodlett-Taylor recalls going to school with Ms. Ellsworth's daughter.

Circa 1952–53, two of the housekeeping staff, Bessie at left and Annie on the right, pose for a visitor's camera. *Courtesy Miami Springs Historical Museum.*

A circa 1951 view of the front of the Miami–Battle Creek main building shows the still imposing facility, complete with the thunderbird emblem on the façade.

An aerial view made after the sale of the former hotel/sanitarium to the South Florida Lutheran Churches shows the immensity of the property. This photo, made in 1980, was part of the publicity done on behalf of the Fair Haven ACLF.

Town of
MIAMI SPRINGS
Florida

November 4th, 1936

TO:
Officers H.E. Frank
        L.K. Cropper:

                    In accordance with ordinance passed
in regular session by the Town Council, Town of Miami Springs,
please notify all residents of the Town as follows:

            I. It will be necessary for all persons em-
ployed as itinerant workers in the town to be registered
and identified.

            2. Residents desiring to recommend persons
employed by them as yardmen, odd job men, or in other capaci-
ties than regular daily employees, should instruct these
presons to report to Mr. J.A. Michael, Town Clerk, Administration Building. Employers should furnish a recommendation
in writing.

            3. Upon identification and investigation, a card
will issued to the employee with a space for signiture of
recommending employer. This card to be carried by the employee while working in the town.

            4. Employers will be notified of any previous
criminal record of employee if such is discovered.

            5. Employers should require to see identifi-
cation card of any unknown person applying for work and
notify Police Department if applicant does not have card.

            6. A Fee of $ .50 will be required to cover
cost of finger-printing and photographing applicants.

            Very truly yours,

            W.D.Kniffin, Marshal

On November 4, 1936, Marshal Kniffin advised his two officers that in accordance with a new town ordinance all itinerant workers employed in Miami Springs would have to be registered, which included being fingerprinted and photographed. "The times, they sure are a-changing!" *Courtesy Miami Springs Historical Museum.*

Maryann Goodlett-Taylor, who grew up in the Springs and is now the city's historian, was a renowned horsewoman. Shown here in 1946 astride her beloved horse Rex, Maryann is one of the many caring and interested citizens who have made a difference in the quality of life in Miami Springs. *Courtesy Maryann Goodlett-Taylor collection.*

Maryann would meet and marry Francis S. Taylor, who became a nationally recognized outdoorsman for whom an Everglades wildlife management area is named. He was the founder of the Taylor Built Airboat, a pioneer in the technology of that form of Everglades travel, and he built the first all-aluminum, riveted airboat. Married in 1949, Maryann was and is justly proud of Francis, who died in 1982 and whose memory is revered almost at the level of Maryann's father and both Glenn Curtiss and James Bright. *Courtesy Maryann Goodlett-Taylor collection.*

On June 29, 1956, these two aerial views were made over Miami Springs, one looking east toward Hialeah, Miami and Biscayne Bay, the other looking southwest from just above Hialeah. While "built up," there was still plenty of room for the city to grow upon.

The north side of Northwest Thirty-sixth Street west of LeJeune Road is part of Miami Springs, and numerous businesses thereon have not only thrived but have also added immeasurably to the city's tax base through the years. Airport Drugs, at 4889 Northwest Thirty-sixth Street, was always a busy place. Shown here on March 18, 1955, well-known pharmacist Moishe Poopick is showing a visiting couple a camera while his bride looks on. Meantime, at the lunch counter, food manager Bill Bailey, just back from home, checks out the day's specials while the waitresses prepare for the lunch rush.

The Miami Airport Motel, at 777 Curtiss Parkway, was a layover for several airlines' crews. Pictured on June 9, 1955, the pool was always a great place to meet stewardesses, known today, of course, as "flight attendants," and now being of both the female and male persuasions.

M & M Cafeteria, a small local Miami chain, had a store at 4471 Northwest Thirty-sixth Street in the International City Building. This picture, made on November 16, 1956, was taken during a lull; the street was ordinarily fraught with traffic.

A marvelous aerial view has us looking northeast from above the old water tower with North Royal Poinciana directly below in the center. The point at which the road curves to the right, shown as a dark shadow, is the former site of the H Bar H Ranch, a great favorite of not only the Springs people, but also of those from Hialeah and surrounding communities. By the time this picture was taken, June 29, 1956, the ranch was already a memory.

There's more to it than meets the eye

MIAMI SPRINGS
Florida

In 1944, the town published this beautiful 5¾-inch by 8¾-inch, sixteen-page booklet extolling the virtues of living in and having a business in Miami Springs. Complete with a fine headshot of Glenn Curtiss, the booklet names the mayor and council and lists all civic clubs including their names and phone numbers. A very rare and highly desirable piece of Miami memorabilia, this is the first and only one that the author has ever seen. *Courtesy Miami Springs Historical Museum.*

Miami Gateway Motel was at East Drive and Northwest Thirty-sixth Street. The swimming pool was a great place to idle away the hours between flights or just for relaxing. Numerous romances began at this now long gone facility.

The Chinese Room of Miami Springs Villas. Owned and managed for many years by the gregarious and always gracious Art Bruns, the hotel was a major meeting and convention facility and was, for many years, the training facility for Eastern Air Lines stewardesses/flight attendants.

As with almost anything else Art Bruns did, the swimming pool at Miami Springs Villas was the largest and most popular of any of the Springs motels. Bruns even went so far as to stage water shows there in competition with the Miami Beach hotels, complete with water clowns and professional swimmers and divers.

Miami Airways Motel, 5055 Northwest Thirty-sixth Street, was another of the inns that was able to capitalize on the numerous flight crew layover schedules, the motel always busy with crews from various airlines coming and going.

A major draw of "the Airways" was the famous Lenny's Hideaway, for years one of Greater Miami's favorite restaurants and one of the first to feature a high-quality buffet. A terrific place to bring a date, Lenny's was one of the busiest dining spots in the area.

Another of the longtime Springs favorites was the restaurant of that name—The Springs—located at 1 Westward Drive, right at the beginning of the circle. Complete with full bar, The Springs featured Maine lobsters and other delicacies.

Miami Springs is blessed with a magnificent country club and golf course, which it finally took ownership of seventy-four years after Glenn Curtiss had sold the land to the City of Miami. Much to its credit, Miami did maintain it as the Miami Springs Country Club for all those years. Now under the management of Carlos Santana, the club is a welcoming and delightful rendezvous for dining as well as, of course, the great game of golf.

This tidy home, at 300 Canal Street, is shown on October 29, 1953. Canal Street fronts the Miami River Canal, and the backyard of the home faced Okeechobee Road in Hialeah.

On March 12, 1956, this was the view at the corner of La Villa and Eastward Drive, the scene quite similar today.

The area of Palmetto and Thirty-seventh Street, one block off of Thirty-sixth Street, was photographed on December 5, 1956. This is one of the few known extant photos of that area of the Springs.

The Miami Springs Police Department is a superbly managed organization under the direction of Chief H. Randall Dilling. Among its forty-three sworn officers are K-9 Officer Albert Sandoval, shown here with his partner Grando, and the motorcycle unit, composed of, from left, Officers Jeff Collins and Jeff Clark, Lieutenant Peter Baan and Officer Robert Berrios. *Both courtesy City of Miami Springs.*

**Miami Springs
Police Department**

201 Westward Drive
Miami Springs, Florida 33166
305/888-9711
24/7

Community Policing Office

274 Westward Drive
Miami Springs, Florida 33166
305/888-5286
M-F 8am-4pm

www.miamispringspolice.com

THE CITY OF

MIAMI SPRINGS

FLORIDA

**Miami Springs
Police Department**

T.I.P.S.

**Tourist
Information** *for*
**Prevention &
Safety**

The police department interacts strongly with the community, and to help ensure the safety and well-being of the numerous visitors to the city, the department publishes this brochure, called "T.I.P.S." Standing for "Tourist Information for Prevention and Safety," the three-panel brochure, printed on both sides, is complete with a series of pointers useful for both tourists and the city's residents to help them avoid crime anywhere they may travel.

Completely conscious of both its and the city's fabled histories, Miami Springs Elementary School, to celebrate its seventieth anniversary, invited the community to join in for a celebratory program on May 2, 2007, complete with a reception following the wonderful event.

Curtiss NC-4 Flying Boat - 1st to cross the Atlantic in 1919, (8 years before Lindbergh)

Learn more visit the

MIAMI SPRINGS HISTORICAL MUSEUM

History of Glenn Hammond Curtiss,
Airline & Aircraft History,
History of Miami Springs, Hialeah
& Opa-Locka

OPEN

Tuesday, Thursday & Saturday
11 a.m. to 4 p.m.

2nd Monday of month
5 p.m. to 8 p.m.

The Miami Springs Historical Museum, sponsored in part by a caring and forward-looking citizenry and city council, is open three days a week and by appointment. Containing an incredible collection of Curtiss-Bright cities historical memorabilia, the new location, at 26 Westward Drive, is accessible from anywhere in south Florida. The museum is a mecca for anybody seeking information on its subject matter, which is shown on the brochure's cover, and visitors are always warmly welcomed by a caring and dedicated all-volunteer staff.

James R. "Jim" Borgmann is Miami Springs' city manager and has spent nearly his entire life in the city he loves. He has served on the council and as assistant city manager, and his life and work are dedicated to Miami Springs. The city's employees and residents hold him in the highest esteem.

Completing five years as chief of police, H. Randall Dilling, upon retirement in 2008, will leave behind a legacy of honor, integrity and high-quality department management.

Former vice-mayor, Councilman Bob Best.

Councilman Paul Dotson.

Councilman Zavier Garcia.

Councilman Rob Youngs.

Miami Springs Mayor William J. "Billy" Bain was born in
Sharon, Pennsylvania, in 1956, and in 1958 his family moved
to Virginia Gardens, where he lived for the next twenty-six
years. In 1984 Billy moved to the Springs, and like so many
others, he found himself swept up in the activities of the
community. A graduate of Miami Springs High School,
Bain has become the city's number one booster, and his love
of place and pride in his hometown of twenty-four years is
evident in everything he says and does that is connected with
Miami Springs.

Five

Opa Locka

What a dream! What an incredible fantasy! And that, of course, is what Opa Locka was originally meant to be. Based on meetings and discussions with developers, architects and planners, who were competing with each other during Florida's real estate boom of the early to mid-1920s, and attempting to differentiate themselves with unique ideas to set their creations apart on the flat south Florida terrain, it appears that Bernhardt Muller, a New York architect, might have come up with the concept of designing a theme town based on settings from tales of Araby. Other sources, however, have differing versions of the story!

It is possible that Curtiss himself, after having read an updated edition of *The Thousand and One Nights*, was inspired by the idea and directed the architects to plan a town based on the theme. In 1925 Curtiss formed the Opa-Locka Company. However, yet another story on Opa Locka's origins has surfaced! In 1976, Frank S. Fitzgerald-Bush wrote his *A Dream of Araby*, a definitive history of the city, and according to Fitzgerald-Bush, his mother gave Curtiss the idea for the city's theme. When Curtiss showed Mrs. Bush, who was the wife of a builder who was also the electrical contractor for Curtiss's development, the town site with its unspoiled native hammocks and detailed his plans for a new city, she supposedly exclaimed, "Oh, Glenn, it's like a dream from the *Arabian Nights*!" This story, which is in *A Dream of Araby*, concludes with a statement that Muller's first proposal for the new town or city was to be in the English Tudor style, a concept that Mr. Curtiss dismissed in favor of the idea that Mrs. Bush is alleged to have inspired.

In any event, after poring over drawings, stories and endless proposals for the city, Muller, with his wife's assistance, began the task of creating the reality from the fantasy that Curtiss was so interested in. Perhaps the single most ambitious part of the project was the Opa-Locka Company's administration building, which, in August 1926, was ready for occupancy. For some years thereafter, until it became uninhabitable due to lack of maintenance in the early years of this century, it served as city hall.

Antolin Garcia Carbonell, in his marvelous 2002 study of the history of the Opa Locka Airport, states that Curtiss originally purchased the property that he would call the Country Club section of Opa Locka, and on which he would build a golf course, from the Tatum Land Company (likely the Tatum Brothers of Miami and Miami Beach fame) on April 27, 1918. The Opa-Locka Company was founded on December 11, 1925, and on January 20, 1926, Charles R. Welch, a salesman for the company, began selling Opa Locka property on-site, with busses bringing prospective buyers up from the company's Flagler Street location in downtown Miami.

On May 14, 1926, Opa Locka was chartered as a town by twenty-eight registered voters who elected John E. Secord as mayor, H.S. Conklin as town marshal and R.A. Samson as town clerk. Shortly thereafter, September 17 and 18 would bring the onslaught of that fabled hurricane, but because of how far inland Opa Locka was, there was no tidal surge and the winds, coming that far over land, were somewhat diminished. The Curtiss-Bright Corporation repaired the damage and opened the planned swimming pool and archery range on schedule.

On Saturday, January 8, 1927, the day Frank Fitzgerald-Bush refers to as "the highwater mark in the town's success," the first southbound trip of the new, all-Pullman sleeping car train, the Orange Blossom Special, stopped at the brand-new Opa Locka station en route to Hialeah and Miami as part of the community's Arabian Nights Fantasy Festival. Turbaned sheiks on snow-white horses greeted the train, and Seaboard Railway President S. Davies Warfield, along with Florida Governor John Martin, alighted to the cheers of the crowd, being welcomed with proclamations and thanked for their faith in Florida, particularly Opa Locka.

For a good few years, Opa Locka would manage to hold its own. Mr. Curtiss's last act on behalf of the city was to give the U.S. Navy the small airfield that had been part of his original purchase. The field was commissioned in January 1931, and in 1938 the base, which was a naval reserve station, was enlarged. Fitzgerald-Bush decried that event, for the navy annexed the old golf course and the old hammock, including the sixty-acre portion of it set aside by Mr. Curtiss for a park. "Bulldozers," writes Fitzgerald-Bush, "levelled the ancient oaks, destroying what had been one of the loveliest natural areas in the county."

World War II would provide an excellent economic foundation for the city, as the several airports located in or adjacent to the community accounted for a large number of jobs, both military and civilian. However, the end of the war and the subsequent closing of all except the Opa Locka Airport (now a civilian field and the U.S. Coast Guard Opa Locka air base) would have severe negative effects upon the city.

Opa Locka today, with its 4.2 square miles and approximately fifteen thousand people, is a working-class community bonded by common goals and interests. Presided over by Mayor Joseph L. Kelley and Vice-mayor Dorothy "Dottie" Johnson, the commission, composed of Rose Tydus, Timothy Holmes and Gale E. Miller, works arduously to improve living conditions and opportunities for the city's residents. City Manager Jannie R. Beverly has earned kudos for his innovative plans and management skills, and the future, while not being problem-free, looks brighter for Opa Locka than it has in many years.

Opa Locka City Hall, 1929. An exotic and glamorous design, the entire city was originally planned to be modeled on the Arabian nights theme, but time, the tides, the military and other changes have had a less than positive effect, and the city is now working hard to overcome some of the negative perceptions that it has been burdened with. *Courtesy Glenn H. Curtiss Museum.*

A late 1930s or early 1940s view of the building shows it from a different angle.

While the name of the event shown in this photograph has been lost to history, the photo clearly shows a very early—1920s, most likely—Opa Locka, complete with attendees dressed in costumes appropriate to the Arabian nights theme.

Curtiss had great plans for the city, and a beautiful and elaborate natatorium was one of the great draws. Shown here in 1925, the city's swimming pool must have been the site that day for some major water-oriented event, judging by the number of cars in the parking lot. *Courtesy Miami Springs Historical Musuem.*

Architectural Drawings: Arabian Fantasies for

OPA-LOCKA

Published by the University of Miami in 1992 for a special exhibition of the original Opa Locka drawings, this booklet is a major resouce for any Curtiss-Bright cities historian or, indeed, any Glenn Curtiss aficionado, as it contains not only a good few images of the drawings but also a great deal of information about Curtiss and his city. *Courtesy of the Glenn H. Museum.*

For many years, Opa Locka was a city of festivals and parades, a "let's have a party" kind of town, possibly due in no small part to the large military presence there. These three May 29, 1955 photographs capture that spirit in the year's Arabian Nights parade.

The yearly Children's Parade was always held shortly before the Arabian Nights parade, likely in order to get the whole city into the spirit of the events. Shown here on May 27, 1955, the astute reader/viewer will note that all of the children in the parade are wearing Arabian-themed headpieces.

Generally the year's parade and festival events began with the city's Lions Club celebrating their trip to the state convention with a gala—including the obligatory parade—early in May. Shown here on May 14, 1955, city and club officials prepare their presentation to state Lions Club leaders upon their arrival in St. Petersburg.

With Ernie Skog's Photo Studio and Camera Shop, Williams Jeweler, Grable's Bakery and Jack's Shoes in the background, the scooter unit of the club passes the reviewing stand.

The May 14, 1955 parade featured, as each year's event did, the Miss Opa Locka Lions Club contest. Regretfully, the beautiful girl on the float is not named, but, most certainly, she should have gone on to state—if not national—honors.

"The harem" poses during the gala event. The sign on the scooter at the left indicates that Opa Locka would be the site of the annual Arabian Nights pageant, May 26–28, 1955.

On July 4, 1954, the Miss Opa Locka Pageant was held, and the beautiful blonde on the right was that year's winner.

Never a city to miss an opportunity to have fun, the Opa Locka of the 1940s through the early '60s was, as far as many were concerned, a great place to enjoy and engage in revelry. In March 1956, Miller's Carnival set up in Opa Locka (as it did for many years) possibly where the Hialeah–Opa Locka Flea Market is today. Shown on March 18, 1956, the carnival was complete with rides, games, midway and a girlie show.

Two of Opa Locka's longtime businesses were Bowman and Bundy Auto Service at 241 Opa Locka Boulevard (January 13, 1955) and Mack's Auto Parts at 2382 Ali Baba Avenue (January 16, 1957).

Marine Drugs, at 391 Opa Locka Boulevard, was shown in the background in a previous Lions Club scooter unit photograph. But this picture, taken on June 7, 1955, is all the more fascinating because of the two dairy trucks that date from a time when home delivery was the norm. The truck parked head-in is from the Land O' Sun Dairy, while the truck parallel to the building on the corner is a MacArthur Dairies truck, that company still in business today.

As it was in almost every other neighborhood, the Dairy Queen at 875 Fisherman Avenue was a great gathering spot for families, especially on warm summer nights, as everybody enjoyed a DQ treat, particularly "the cone with the curl on top." (February 12, 1955)

Two of Opa Locka's several inns were the Opa Locka Hotel, on the Boulevard of the same name, and the Cris Cros Motel at 141 Sharazad Boulevard. Owned by Mr. and Mrs. Gaetano Longo, the Cris Cros was a favorite of truckers avoiding the higher prices closer to downtown Miami.

This picture of the Pine Tree Apartments at 1111 Sharazad Boulevard was taken on August 26, 1955, and shows a lovely peaceful apartment house similar to those on (for example) Biscayne Beach, Miami Beach.

On July 13, 1957, the corner of Fisherman and Nomad Streets shows a typical prosperous Dade County middle-class neighborhood.

Another view of Fisherman and Nomad Streets on July 13, 1957, gives a different view of the area, showing the water tanks of one of the airports in the background on the right between the two tall trees.

Yet a third view of the Fisherman and Nomad Streets shows a dry cleaning store in the background on the right, the cars certainly indicative of a working-class neighborhood.

Two absolutely incredible views show the changes and contrasts between "then" and "now." The scene with the traffic light is at the intersection of Northwest 27th Avenue and 131st Street on June 25, 1963, while the view on Northwest 135th Street looks west toward the Seaboard Railway tracks on December 8, 1961. Neither location is recognizable today, as 27th Avenue is now eight lanes wide at that point, while 135th Street is six lanes wide.

OLD SCANDIA'S
FAMOUS SMÖRGÅSBORD
OPPOSITE CITY HALL. OPA LOCKA. FLORIDA

Opa Locka's (and one of Greater Miami's) favorite restaurant for many years was Old Scandia, owned by Mr. and Mrs. H. Johansen and operated as a Danish smorgasbord restaurant, the only one in the county until Prince Hamlet opened some years later. At 125 Perviz Avenue, opposite city hall, the restaurant was nationally renowned and the food was superb. After Mrs. Johansen died, Mr. J. lost interest and the restaurant began a long, slow decline, eventually closing in the late 1970s.

For the dragsters Opa Locka Speedway was one of the most exciting venues in the Miami area, and one of its regular racers was David Smith. His stories of the races and the people are the stuff of legends. David is shown here carrying the flag to start a race and driving "May Win," the May referring to May Nelson, wife of the Nelson's Garage owner. The wreck photo shows David's car, #77, after its last race. As he related to the author, "this one hurt and it was the end of my circle track racing!" *Courtesy of David Y. Smith and Valerie Caracappa.*

Two views of Opa Locka Boulevard in the mid-1970s show it under construction and being upgraded, the street at that time very much like the Opa Locka of today, a work in progress with a tough road ahead, but given the opportunity to overcome its problems, a great future.

Six

By Train and Plane to the Curtiss-Bright Cities

The Florida East Coast Railway arrived on the shores of Biscayne Bay on April 15, 1896, its first passenger train arriving one week later on April 22. While Hialeah Park would enjoy service from downtown Miami on the FEC's racetrack specials beginning in 1924, none of the Curtiss-Bright cities would see a mainline through passenger train until January 8, 1927, when the Seaboard's Orange Blossom Special would make its first trip south from New York and stop in both Opa Locka and Hialeah en route to Miami.

Miami Springs was in an interesting position. The FEC's Hialeah Belt line crossed the Miami River Canal on its way to Hialeah Yard, staying just north of Miami Springs, which even with the addition of the 1954–55 annexation would still not give the Springs rail service. Patrons who wished to take the train to points north or west in Florida or the rest of the country needed to travel to the Hialeah station of the Seaboard or the downtown Miami FEC station in order to enjoy rail service.

When the FEC planned the great Kissimmee Valley Extension, the line was scheduled to come down from South Bay, on the south side of Lake Okeechobee, using a right of way that would take it through what would years later become Pennsuco, and then farther south into beautiful downtown Medley and directly into Hialeah Yard. Geographically, the yard was neither in Hialeah nor Miami Springs, but, rather, across the canal that is on the west side of the Springs and Virginia Gardens and which separates the latter community from the railroad yard.

The yard opened in 1925, complete with light repair facilities and a large brick roundhouse, but with the onset of the Depression it was closed by the railroad and used only for the storage of unneeded steam locomotives. The line into Hialeah branched off from the FEC mainline just south of Northeast Seventy-ninth Street in Miami, then went west into the yard and north into, through and a bit north of Medley. That line was all that remained—at the time—of the never completed Kissimmee Valley Extension.

On January 22, 1963, the nonoperating employees of the FEC went on strike, and shortly thereafter the railroad discontinued its passenger service and reopened Hialeah Yard, moving all operations out of the downtown Miami area. Today, Hialeah Yard, still in unincorporated Dade County, is a major employer of those living in Virginia Gardens and the Springs and an equally major generator of business for Miami Springs.

Although the Opa Locka station was closed shortly after Amtrak took over all U.S. railroad passenger services on May 1, 1971, Hialeah's passenger and freight depot, which had served the Seaboard Railway and its successors since January 1927, remained active. Today, although not seeing any through passenger trains, the depot serves numerous Tri-Rail commuter trains on a daily basis. The Amtrak station moved from its longtime Northwest Seventh Avenue location (near downtown) to a site adjacent to the CSX Transportation Company (formerly Seaboard Coast Line Railroad) yard that is located just outside of Hialeah at Northwest Eighty-third Street and Thirty-sixth Avenue. Patrons can utilize that station for Amtrak's service to the northeast.

And what of the airlines? At one time the Curtiss-Bright cities boasted five airports, including All-American Field (also known as Masters Field, which was, according to Antolin G. Carbonell—author of the marvelous study titled *The History of Opa Locka Airport*—for a very brief time in 1941 the original Miami International Airport), Miami Municipal Airport, Opa Locka Airport, the Marine Corps Air Station (which was actually within the Opa Locka Naval Air Station facility) and today's Miami International Airport, which, though not in Miami Springs, is directly across Northwest Thirty-sixth Street. All of these fields have played important parts in the area's general and aviation history, and Opa Locka Airport remains active today. Miami-Dade College North campus is now on the site of the Marine Corps Air Station, while UPS's main Miami facility is where Masters Field once was and is also where Amelia Earhart took off from on her ill-fated flight.

There are varying dates for the first arrival of an airplane in the Curtiss-Bright cities, but one of the prime candidates is that of Colonel A.R. McMullen, who it appears flew into a real estate subdivision in Hialeah (possibly Deer Park) and even avoided hitting the stakes. According to the eyewitness accounts, McMullen was told that, at that time, the Miami area had no operating aviation facilities although barnstorming was, in the outlying areas, already popular.

Suffice to say that, obviously, the history of the various airports in the Curtiss-Bright cities would take up a large book, but in way of summation, all commercial flights were eventually consolidated at Miami International Airport directly south of Miami Springs. Opa Locka Airport has remained a major charter and private aircraft landing field with important services managed by fixed base operators. Additionally, the U.S. Coast Guard flies untold numbers of flights from the same airport, that part of the field being known as the U.S. Coast Guard base Opa Locka, its future secure because of its strategic location astride the air and sea routes connecting Miami with Latin America.

An incredibly rare photograph, likely made by an onlooker with a box camera, shows the January 20, 1926 groundbreaking for the Seaboard Railway Extension from West Palm Beach to Homestead via Opa Locka, Hialeah and Miami. *From left*: Hialeah Mayor Grethen; John M. Bowman, president of the Bowman–Biltmore Hotel in Coral Gables; E.G. Foley, contracting company president; S. Davies Warfield, Seaboard Railway president; and Coral Gables Mayor Edward E. "Doc" Dammers (in shirt sleeves) turned the first shovels of earth at Hialeah.

Standing in front of the locomotive for publicity photographs after the Orange Blossom Special reached Hialeah on January 8, 1927, are, from left, Miss Hialeah, Seaboard President Warfield, Miss Miami, Florida Governor John W. Martin and, it is thought, Mrs. Martin.

On January 8, 1927, the first trip of the all-Pullman sleeping car Orange Blossom Special is welcomed with daylong festivities at Opa Locka and Hialeah, stopping at each city en route to its Miami terminal. The locomotive is festooned with flowers and bunting, the train name proudly displayed on the front of the boiler below the headlight.

In December 1938, the Seaboard inaugurated diesel-electric-powered streamliner service between Pennsylvania Station, Manhattan and Miami, naming the train the Silver Meteor. Celebrating its millionth mile of operation on November 10, 1940, the train broke through the celebratory sign, which was placed just north of the Hialeah depot. *Photograph from Romer Collection, Miami–Dade Public Library.*

Until the July 1, 1967 merger of the Seaboard with the Atlantic Coast Line Railroad, most Seaboard secondary trains stopped at the Opa Locka depot. Shown on November 11, 1970, the depot later suffered several fires but has since been restored and is a regular stop for Tri-Rail trains en route between the Miami International Airport station and West Palm Beach.

Photographed from the air in the early 1960s the Seaboard Railway yard includes storeroom, repair and general maintenance facilities. The overpass directly ahead is East 49th Street in Hialeah, Northwest 103rd Street in Miami. Hialeah is directly to the left and looking farther north one can see, at right, the U.S. Marine Corps Air Station, now Miami-Dade College's north campus. At left is Masters Field, today the main Miami depot of UPS, just south of which is the new and modern Hialeah Police headquarters.

This one of a kind photograph was taken in the mid- to late 1960s and shows, at upper right, to the left of the tracks, the Seaboard's Hialeah station, complete with a long passenger train passing by. The expressway is State Road 112. The street at lower left is Northwest North River Drive, and Northwest Thirty-sixth Street runs from left to right in front of the expressway and is blocked by the train. While the view today has changed dramatically, the Seaboard station is still in place and still serves passenger trains of the commuter railroad Tri-Rail.

Opposite: This 1937–38 picture is one of the rarest Florida railroad photographs ever made, for it shows the building controlling Hialeah Junction, which was just south of the Hialeah depot and was the point at which trains heading into Miami's passenger station diverged from the line that went into the old yard (which was actually between two runways at Miami Airport!).

Following the strike by nonoperating employees against the Florida East Coast Railway, which began on January 22, 1963, the FEC moved its operations to Hialeah Yard. By order of the Florida Supreme Court, the FEC was required to resume passenger service between North Miami and Jacksonville on August 2, 1965. On August 1, 1965, the author, the only "railroad buff" allowed on FEC property during the strike, and now the official company historian, photographed the passenger train, headed by an E9A-type diesel-electric locomotive at Hialeah Yard. Though originating and terminating at the yard, the passenger train did not carry passengers or make any stops between the yard and North Miami depot.

Opposite, top: There are few rarer aviation images extant than this incredible view made on May 15, 1934, as the dirigible USS *Macon* left Opa Locka for its Sunnyvale, California base. Along with the spectacular vista, complete with the dirigible's landing field below, the cancellation, made on May 16, 1934, adds to the incredible rarity of this piece.

Opposite, bottom: One of the few names in commercial aviation to have reached legendary status, besides Curtiss, the Wright Brothers, Amelia Earhart and Juan T. Trippe of Pan-American, is Eddie Rickenbacker. "Captain Eddie," for many years president of Eastern Air Lines and the driving force behind the company until it was taken over by incompetents and run into the ground, is shown here in his hat deplaning from a DC-6 at Miami International Airport just prior to the jet age. Of note is the open walkway, which was part of the terminal, behind and below the wing.

OPA LOCKA BIDS THE U.S.S. MACON
BON VOYAGE AND HAPPY LANDINGS
ON ITS RETURN TRIP TO SUNNYVALE

The Opa Locka Marine Air Base, December 17, 1954. The control tower, while not visible in this photo, is currently being used for offices by Miami-Dade College and one of the large hangar buildings was also converted for use by the school, which is located at Northwest 27th Avenue and 119th Street. That street—Northwest 119th—runs right through what was part of the airfield.

Opposite, top: A Pan-American Stratoclipper is taking off from Miami, the old terminal building sign in the left background. Until 1952, when the Seaboard moved its yard from the site of today's Miami International Airport (MIA) to a larger location between Northwest 83rd and Northwest 103rd Streets, the yard was between two runways at what is now MIA. The Port Authority finally arranged to swap land with the railroad so that they could move their operations and the airport could be expanded.

Opposite, bottom: A late 1940s view of MIA shows an Eastern Air Lines two-engine Silver Falcon in front of the old terminal, a National Airlines plane behind it and three Pan Am planes farther west on the tarmac. The old MIA was both busy and congested, and in 1960 a new terminal opened with its entrance fronting LeJeune Road (Northwest Forty-second Avenue). "Thirty-sixth Street Airport" was closed, and for a few years the businesses along that street went through a period of decline. Little by little, though, as MIA became busier and busier, the street made a comeback and today is again a major business street, filled with commercial stores, restaurants and motels, including the Miami Springs Villas.

D259:—PAN AMERICAN STRATOCLIPPER, MIAMI, FLORIDA

M-15—Miami's International Airport
Gateway to Latin American Countries

An Eastern DC-4 readies for departure from MIA in 1947. With a cloudy sky the four-engine prop plane could be in for a bumpy departure.

With the new terminal and its hotel in the background, a Pan-American jet clipper awaits instructions from the tower before taxiing out onto the runway in 1962.

In closing our chapter on "getting there" we end with an incredible view: the Florida East Coast Railway overpass of Okeechobee Road, which opened in 2005 after years of planning and cooperation between the railway, the city of Hialeah, the county and the state. The FEC's numerous freight trains to and from Hialeah Yard now no longer have to cross the busy six-lane U.S. 27 as many as twenty-four times each day. Motorists are reminded daily that they are passing below the tracks of America's most exciting and best-managed railroad.

Seven

Gardens in the Neighborhood

The story of the Curtiss-Bright cities would not be complete without a look at the two neighboring communities, Virginia Gardens and Hialeah Gardens, the former bordering on and once a part of Miami Springs, the latter, of course, adjacent to Hialeah's northwest boundaries.

The Village of Virginia Gardens, which is, size-wise, one of Miami–Dade County's smallest municipalities, is bordered by Northwest Thirty-sixth Street on the south, Curtiss Parkway (Northwest Fifth-seventh Avenue, also known as Red Road) on the east, Lafayette Drive on the north and Ludlum Drive and the Ludlum Canal on the west.

Virginia Gardens was born out of the most unlikely of circumstances: the area, then part of Miami Springs, was inhabited primarily by people who had moved south from Virginia. In the mid-1940s, Miami Springs passed an ordinance prohibiting the keeping of horses. What is today's Virginia Gardens was then farmland, which even included a duck farm off of Northwest Sixty-sixth Avenue. Most of the original residents lived on five-acre ranches and owned horses for pleasure and for riding.

The village was incorporated in 1947 and its commission was chartered in 1951. The first mayor, Willam W. Perry, was sworn in on September 17, 1952, and the village charter was approved by the state legislature on July 28, 1953.

The last of Virginia Garden's horses were removed by ordinance in March 1976. On July 4, 1994, Bonilyn Wilbanks was named chief of police, becoming the first female police chief in Dade County and one of only seven in the state. Today the village administration is in the hands of Mayor Spencer Deno, Council President Debra Conover and council members Jorge Arce, Richard Block, Steven K. Petterson and Elizabeth Taylor-Martinez. Chief of Police James Chohonis oversees a department of twenty-three sworn officers including three reserve officers.

Hialeah Gardens borders Hialeah toward the northwest end of the latter city, primarily along Okeechobee Road. Its history began in December 1948, when twelve people met at Youngblood's Filling Station at Walter C. Ohlert's Tourist Camp to found a town. With a unanimous vote, the little community of twenty-six registered voters became the incorporated town of Hialeah Gardens. By January, hats were purchased for police officers and a badge for the town marshal. February brought the adoption of the first building code, building permit and inspection fee; the first laws regulating hunting; and the first traffic ordinance. One year later, the Land Use and Zoning Master Plan was adopted to plan the growth of a city that until 1968 was primarily a rural community where raising horses was one of the main industries, with only a limited number of small businesses along Okeechobee Road.

Today, the city's location and proximity to major roadways has allowed Hialeah Gardens to become one of the fastest growing and most vital municipalities in Miami–Dade County, with a population of over twenty thousand residents. The mayor of Hialeah Gardens is Yioset de la Cruz, and the council consists of Luciano "Lucky" Garcia, Rolando "Roly" Pina, Jorge A. Merida, Elmo L. Urra and Jorge Gutierrez. An emphasis on providing and maintaining open spaces for parks and recreational activities and the development of beautiful residential areas combined with a well-planned and regulated commercial community continue to make Hialeah Gardens an ideal place to call home.

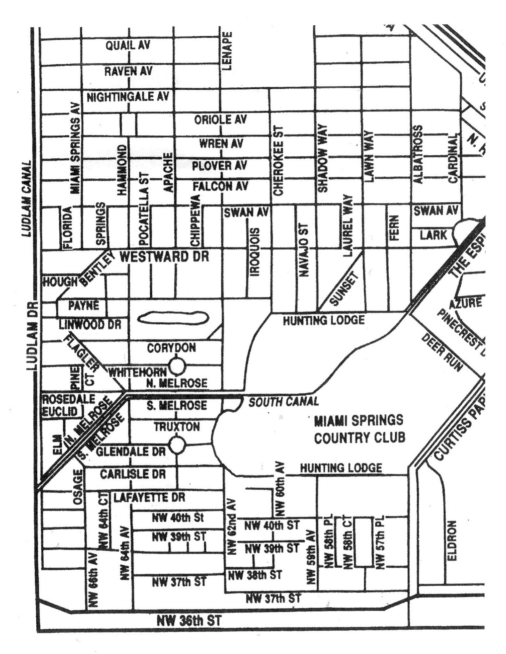

As described above, the boundaries of Virginia Gardens can be seen on this map, with Northwest Thirty-sixth Street marking the southern boundary at bottom and Lafayette Drive as the north village limit only six blocks north. On an east-west bias the village runs from Curtiss Parkway to the point at which Lafayette Drive would intersect if it were a through street, while Ludlum Drive and the Ludlum Canal mark the village boundaries on the west.

50th Anniversary!

VILLAGE OF VIRGINIA GARDENS
FLORIDA
EST 1947

YESTERDAY . . .
TODAY . . .
TOMORROW . . .

Fifty Years of Memories
1947-1997

To celebrate its fiftieth anniversary, in 1997 the village issued this beautiful 6⅞-inch by 8½-inch, forty-page, heavy stock cover booklet. An excellent primer on the village's history and accomplishments, this booklet is a fine collectible for anybody interested in the history and background of one of Greater Miami's smaller and too often overlooked municipalities.

A modern progressive city, Hialeah Gardens has recently moved forward with new and updated municipal facilities. The city hall, under construction, is shown here. *Courtesy City of Hialeah Gardens.*

In 1959, Hialeah Gardens was still a town and was, for all intents and purposes, "out in the boonies." Today, of course, adjacent to Hialeah, the city is easily reached from anywhere in Greater Miami, but, as can be seen in this 1959 photograph, the street is being paved so that the few police cars could have easier access to the police station. Courtesy City of Hialeah Gardens.

Today's modern Hialeah Gardens Police Station is a far cry from the building that housed the department in 1959. Under the direction of Chief Van Toth, the department now has thirty sworn officers and twelve civilian employees and is in step with the use of updated police technology. *Courtesy City of Hialeah Gardens.*

In closing, the author salutes the five municipalities covered in this volume, along with their employees and their residents, who, present and past, are responsible for building the wonderful village and the four great cities discussed herein. By including this view of the Hialeah Police Honor Guard, it is my hope that each and every person in the five communities will know what an honor it has been for me to have had the opportunity to present that history. The Curtiss-Bright cities and the "gardens in the neighborhood" are some of the finest places in America in which to live, work and raise a family. *Courtesy City of Hialeah.*